THE TRAVEL ENRICHMENT SERIES

SOUTH PACIFIC

12 TALES TO ENLIGHTEN YOUR JOURNEY

James Grant-Peterkin

JGP

1st Edition 2023

Design by Marjorie Dotte

ISBN: 978-956-416-094-8
Intellectual Property: 192.178

Contents

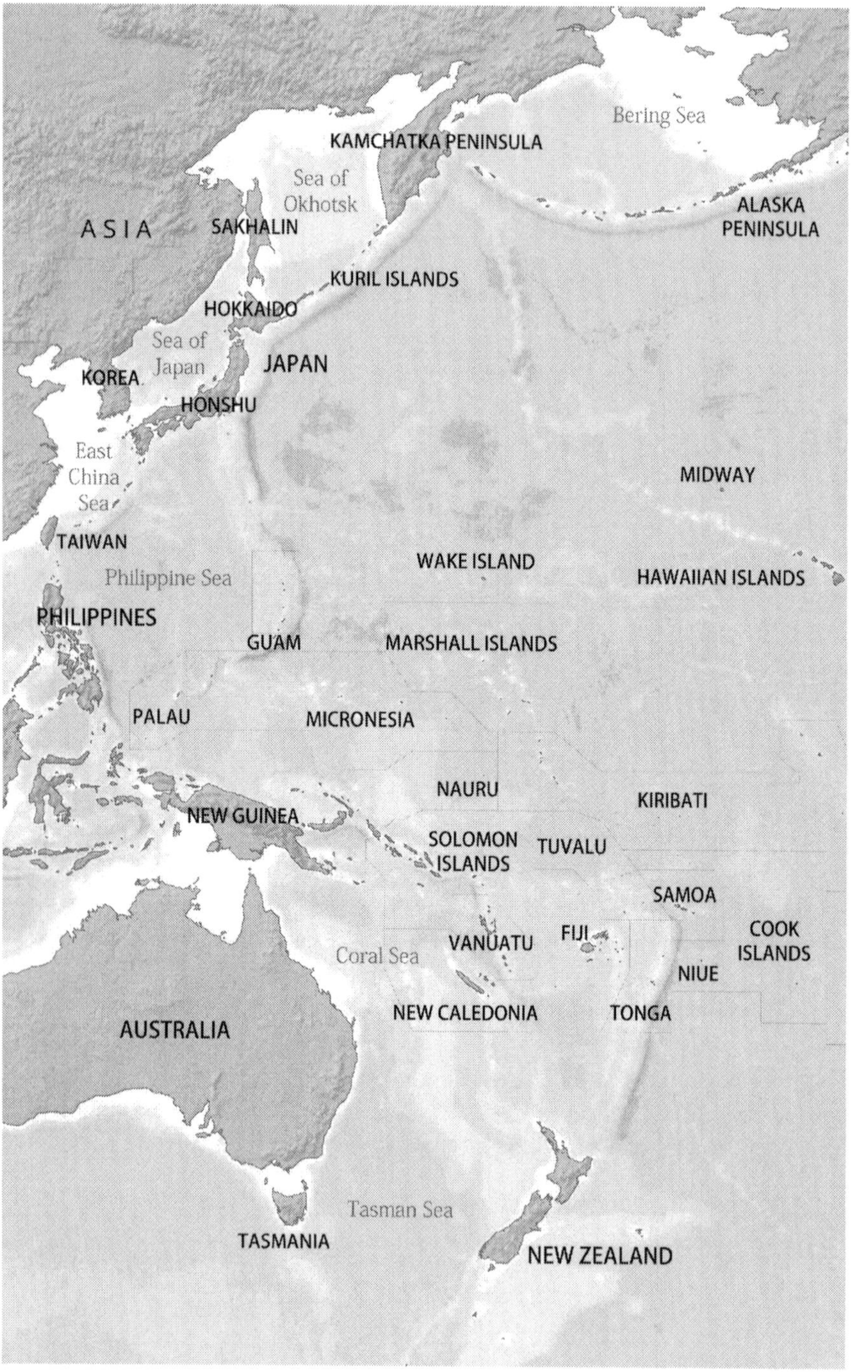
Bering Sea
KAMCHATKA PENINSULA
Sea of Okhotsk
ALASKA PENINSULA
ASIA
SAKHALIN
KURIL ISLANDS
HOKKAIDO
Sea of Japan
JAPAN
KOREA
HONSHU
East China Sea
MIDWAY
TAIWAN
WAKE ISLAND
Philippine Sea
HAWAIIAN ISLANDS
PHILIPPINES
GUAM
MARSHALL ISLANDS
PALAU
MICRONESIA
NAURU
KIRIBATI
NEW GUINEA
SOLOMON ISLANDS
TUVALU
SAMOA
COOK ISLANDS
FIJI
VANUATU
Coral Sea
NIUE
NEW CALEDONIA
TONGA
AUSTRALIA
Tasman Sea
TASMANIA
NEW ZEALAND

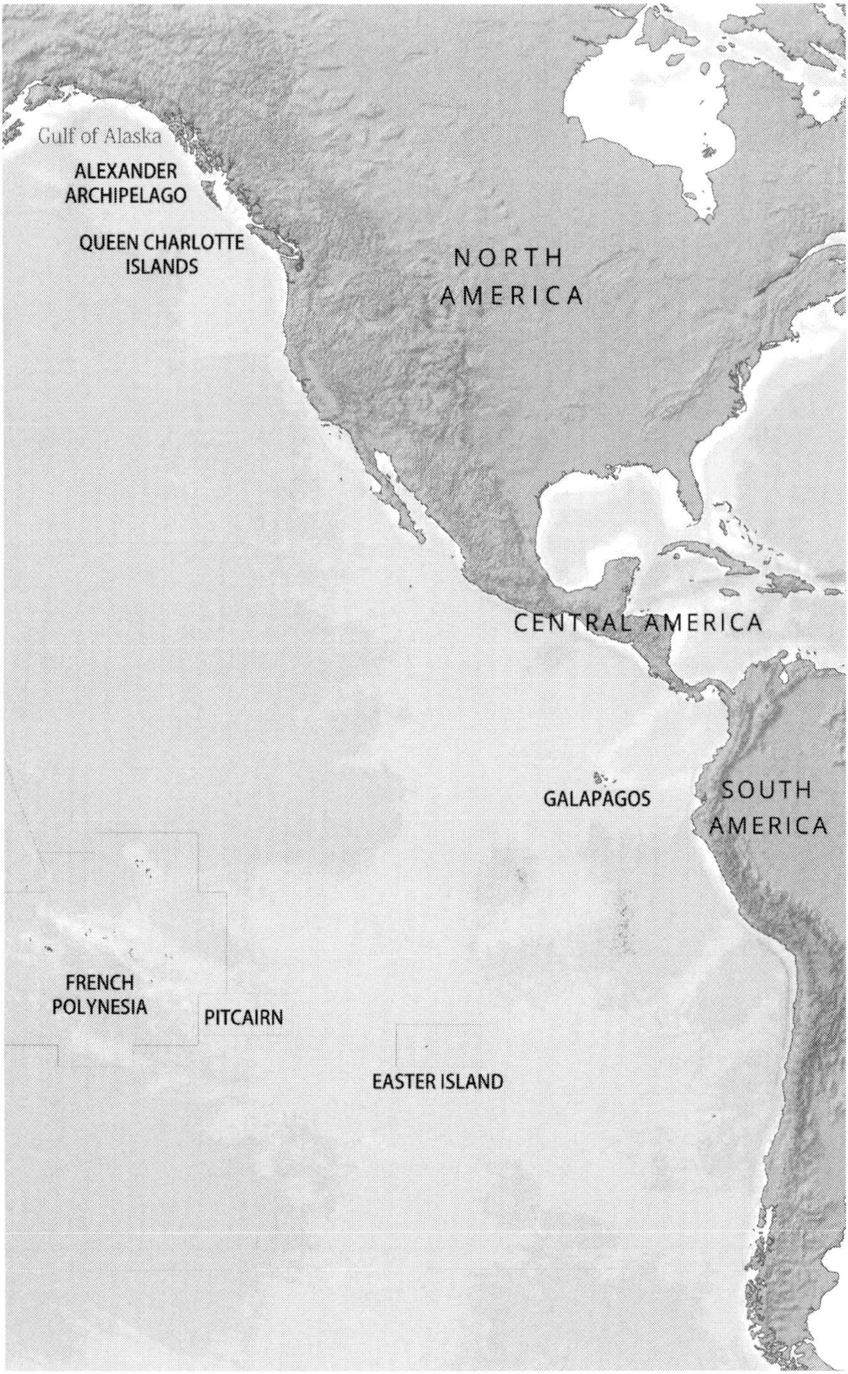
Gulf of Alaska
ALEXANDER ARCHIPELAGO
QUEEN CHARLOTTE ISLANDS
NORTH AMERICA
CENTRAL AMERICA
GALAPAGOS
SOUTH AMERICA
FRENCH POLYNESIA
PITCAIRN
EASTER ISLAND

Introduction

'[Tahiti] is the land of Venus reborn … I thought I was transported into the Garden of Eden. We found companies of men and women sitting under the shade of their fruit-trees. Everywhere we found hospitality, ease, innocent joy, and every appearance of happiness among them.'

– Louis Antoine de Bougainville (1771)

Ever since de Bougainville penned this poetic description of Tahiti during his successful circumnavigation of the world, so the utopian image of the South Pacific was born, and little has changed in the intervening 250 years. Spanning almost one third of the globe and stretching all the way from the Arctic Circle to Antarctica, the Pacific is the world's largest and deepest ocean, and contains about 25,000 islands within its boundaries. These islands are home to some of the warmest and most welcoming people on Earth, and it is this hospitality, coupled with the natural beauty of many of the islands, that has kept visitors coming back to the region over and over again. But be warned: there is also an alluring and unexpected magnetism to many of these islands, something that I discovered for myself when I wandered into the South Pacific almost by chance in 1996, and have struggled to leave ever since.

Given the universal appeal of the Pacific Islands, there is a logical tendency for travellers to overlook their cultural and historical qualities in favour of their idyllic beaches and turquoise lagoons, and this strikes me as a shame. Today, the Pacific Ocean is blessed with a rich tapestry of human history, made up of important events that took place on the islands themselves coupled with the actions and achievements of famous visitors. The aim of this book is to offer an introduction to both, in the firm belief that the pleasure we derive from our travels grows in direct proportion to our understanding of the places we visit. In a 21st century travel industry increasingly dominated by selfies and social media, it feels that the need for well-researched background information has never been greater.

The twelve stories contained in this book are a blend of early and more contemporary Pacific history, and each one has been carefully selected based on my own years of living and studying here. The book starts and finishes with two of its most factual narratives, on the basis that it is difficult to understand the Pacific Islands fully without a concise explanation of their settlement, and likewise another one examining the far-reaching effects that the Second World War (WW2) had on the region. The chapters in between offer short biographies of exceptional and engaging characters such as Amelia Earhart and Thor Heyerdahl, together with other more withdrawn ones such as Tom Neale and James Cook, whose own Pacific journal documented little more than the daily weather reports! The protagonists of these tales range from individuals with whom almost everyone is familiar, to others who I hope are completely new to you, with the intention that the chapters can be read independently from each other and in any order.

Most importantly of all, I hope that these stories greatly enhance and enrich your visit to this delightful region.

JGP

1. The Origins of Polynesia

'More than an ocean, the Pacific was like a universe, and a chart of it looked like a portrait of the night sky. This enormous ocean was like the whole of heaven, an inversion of earth and air, so that the Pacific seemed like outer space, an immensity of emptiness, dotted with misshapen islands that twinkled like stars, archipelagos like star clusters, and wasn't Polynesia a sort of galaxy?'

– Paul Theroux

In approximately 4000 BC, a group of islanders from modern-day Taiwan cast off in their canoes and so set in motion the greatest human migration in our planet's history. Some of the descendants of those early Taiwanese explorers, known today as Polynesians, successfully populated nearly every single habitable island in the Pacific Ocean, from the Hawaiian archipelago in the north, to solitary Easter Island (Rapa Nui) in the east, to New Zealand (Aotearoa) in the southwest.

The debate over the greatest seafaring nation in our history has generally focused on the Vikings and their conquest of large swathes of Europe between the 8th and 11th centuries, together with their pioneering voyages to North Africa, the Middle East, and even North America. Three centuries later, sailors from China's Ming Dynasty established new technologies in shipbuilding and navigational know-how to successfully sail their large fleets across Southeast Asia, India, and even as far as the east coast of Africa. However, it is difficult to compare any of these feats with the early voyages of the Polynesians, who explored over 16 million square miles of uncharted ocean and developed navigational techniques that are unimaginable in our modern era of GPS. How they managed to reach almost every far-flung island in the Pacific, and equally importantly, *why* they did so, is the focus of this first chapter.

The descendants of the seafarers who left Taiwan would ultimately sail as far west as Madagascar and as far east as Easter Island, and it is generally accepted that they also reached the west coast of South America, even if they never settled there. Since the thousands of languages spoken within this vast geographical area are all today classified under the single umbrella of **Austronesian**, so the islands that make up Polynesia also form part of this extensive linguistic empire, and can therefore trace their roots all the way back to a common ancestor in Southeast Asia.

The islands of the Pacific Ocean have historically been divided up into three distinct geographical regions, and while these divisions are now nearly 200 years old and not by any means ethnographically perfect, they do help reduce the erroneous belief that all Pacific Islanders are culturally identical. For now, each island in the Pacific is classified into one of the following three sub-regions:

Micronesia: derived from the Greek for 'small islands', this region in the northwest Pacific Ocean retains close cultural and linguistic ties with Southeast Asia. It consists of island nations such as Palau, the Marshall Islands, Guam, and the Federal States of Micronesia. Interestingly, one half of Kiribati (pronounced '*Ki-ri-bas*') is found in Micronesia and the other half in Polynesia.

Melanesia: despite its comparatively small size, Melanesia contains the greatest cultural diversity of the three regions. An extreme example of this is Papua New Guinea (PNG), where over 800 different languages are spoken, going some way to explain why politics in PNG is such a complicated business! The name derives from the Greek for 'dark islands' due to the skin colour of the inhabitants (remember that these names were assigned in the early 19th century, long before this type of categorisation would have been regarded as racially insensitive).

Polynesia: by far the largest of the three regions in terms of geographical area, the name comes from the Greek for 'many islands', and Polynesia contains over 1,000 of them. Due to its shape, it is often referred to as the Polynesian Triangle, with its corners consisting of Hawai'i, Easter Island, and New Zealand. Contained within this triangle are the small island nations of Samoa, Tonga, the Cook Islands, and French Polynesia amongst others. Despite the vast distances separating the island groups (New Zealand and Hawai'i are over 4,500 miles apart), all Polynesians consider themselves to be closely related to each other and descended from a common ancestor. A multi-national gathering of Polynesian islanders is really like one big family reunion, in which people will often refer to each other as 'cousins', despite all hailing from different homelands. Attending an international event such as the Festival of Pacific Arts, which takes place once every four years on a rotational basis around the region, is highly recommended if you'd like to experience this diverse assortment of cultures for yourself.

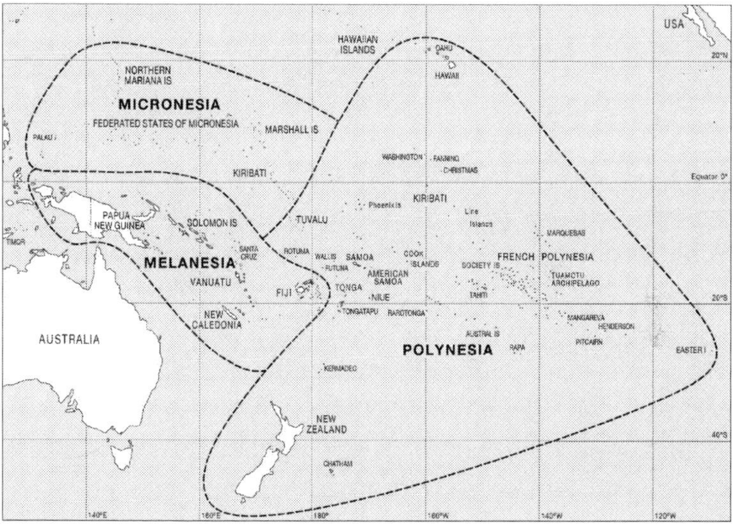

A final word on the names of the region: **Oceania** is the collective term given to the continent of Australia plus all the islands of Polynesia, Melanesia, and Micronesia. Australia alone is one of the seven continents that make up Earth, and is the smallest one in terms of landmass. However, Oceania is not considered to be a continent in itself, although you will sometimes see it included as one instead of Australia, or even as part of Australasia. All very confusing!

The Exploration of an Ocean

The human migration across the Pacific Islands that started in Taiwan gradually spread in a south-easterly direction towards the north coast of PNG and the Solomon Islands. By this time, both Australia and PNG had long been settled by groups of people who had travelled overland from Africa and across Southeast Asia, during an age when the sea levels on Earth were considerably lower and all three continents were still connected by land bridges. The Indigenous Australians were not a seafaring people, and despite the fact that they have now inhabited Australia for well over 60,000 years – long before the Austronesians even existed – there is no evidence that they ever embarked on exploratory voyages into the Pacific.

From the Solomon Islands, the Austronesian expansion continued through the rest of Melanesia, before finally reaching Tonga and Samoa in about 1000 BC. This was the first recorded arrival of men and women into the region that would later become known as Polynesia. A slight pause in the migration occurred at this point, and archaeological studies suggest that it was another 1,000 years before they settled the Cook Islands and Tahiti, in the very heart of the Polynesian triangle. Finally, it was from this central region that the expansion towards the outlying archipelagos took place: Polynesians are thought to have arrived in the Marquesas Islands in about AD 700, reached Pitcairn Island in about AD 800, and discovered the three corners of the Polynesian triangle soon after that: Hawai'i (AD 900), Easter Island (AD 1000), and finally New Zealand (AD 1200).

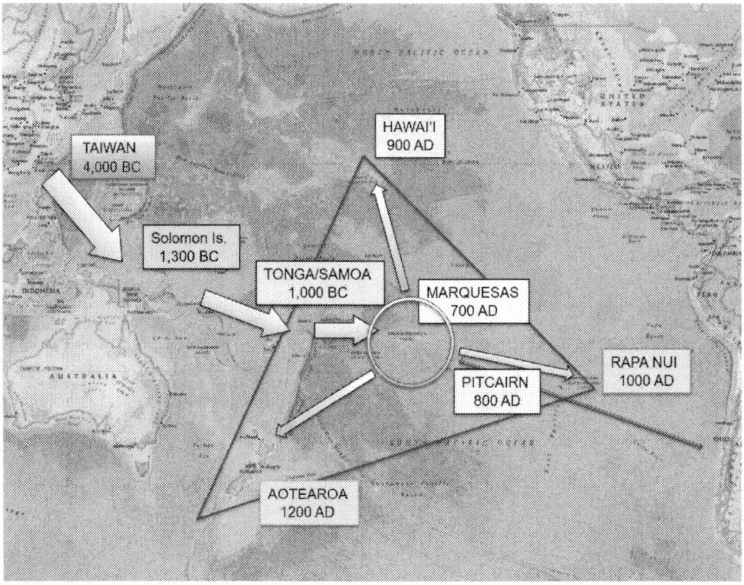

The human settlement of the Pacific took over 5,000 years to complete, in a gradual yet purposeful expansion from west to east. For their exploratory nature and pioneering technologies, these voyages were the equivalent of the early 1960s space missions, and required unprecedented levels of scientific knowledge and expertise. The Polynesians' discovery of New Zealand resulted in the settlement of the last significant landmass on our planet, and yet any suggestion that this far-reaching expansion may have been the product of indiscriminate voyaging fails to appreciate the precision required to locate new islands in the middle of a vast ocean. With some islands separated by thousands of miles from each other, a miscalculation of just one degree during the sea passage could easily have resulted in missing one's destination completely.

Equally impressive was the Polynesians' ability to adapt seamlessly to different environments and conditions, and the same race of people who thrived on isolated coral atolls close to the equator also successfully inhabited Aotearoa (New Zealand), a group of temperate and mountainous continental islands. Similarly, Polynesians flourished equally well on clusters of islands in close proximity to each other as they did on solitary outcrops such as Rapa Nui (Easter Island), which is over 1,000 miles from its nearest inhabited neighbour.

From the East or West?

The fact that we can retrace the route of this extensive migration with any accuracy is thanks in part to pottery. Archaeological excavations in New Caledonia in 1952 revealed for the first time that the people who were gradually expanding across the Pacific were also producing a distinctive type of pottery known as Lapita, and subsequent studies have shown that the Lapita people occupied an area from PNG all the way to Samoa, making them the precursors to the Polynesians. The examination of artefacts unearthed at these sites has helped to explain much about the way of life of these people, and radiocarbon dating has provided much greater clarity regarding when each island was occupied. Nevertheless, archaeologists today continue to disagree over the exact timeframe in which each island in the Pacific was settled, and the dates listed earlier should be taken as general estimations, with an error margin of up to +/-150 years. However, any outstanding questions regarding the direction of the settlement of Polynesia have now all been answered, and extensive studies by scientists from a wide range of disciplines have resulted in unanimous agreement on this point.

The theory that Polynesia may have been settled from South America was proposed by several anthropologists in the first half of the 20th century, based on the fact that the prevailing winds and currents in the South Pacific supported this direction of travel. It was tested most famously in 1947 by the Norwegian explorer Thor Heyerdahl, who aimed to show that indigenous South Americans could have drifted westwards across the Pacific and into Polynesia, and his experiment on board the balsawood raft *Kon-Tiki* is covered in a dedicated chapter later in this book.

How Did They Do It?

The Polynesians were not only highly accomplished navigators, but also perfected the art of designing their canoes for these epic transoceanic voyages. The outrigger, an external float protruding over one or both sides of a boat, was a feature invented by the Austronesians, and this significant addition resulted in faster and more balanced canoes, offering a convenient means of travel between nearby islands. They later developed much larger double-hulled canoes for voyaging across greater distances, thus enabling groups of scouts to explore far beyond the horizon in search of new islands to inhabit. When Captain Cook first visited the South Pacific in 1769, he was astonished by the technical complexity of the Polynesian canoes and was left in no doubt whatsoever that these people were well-established seafarers.

Our understanding of the techniques employed by the Polynesians to navigate across hundreds of miles of empty ocean, without any apparent waypoints or visual cues, is probably only a very basic notion of the actual methods used. There is a common misunderstanding among nonexperts that they merely sailed off in a predominantly easterly direction and chanced upon any new islands in a purely random and haphazard manner. However, while there clearly was a degree of trial and error involved in the process of discovering new lands, the actual settling of them was very definitely a precise form of science. Polynesian scouts were able to explore vast expanses of uncharted waters on the basis that if they hadn't sighted any new land by the halfway point of the food and freshwater that they carried on board with them, they could turn around and make for home, safe in the knowledge that the return journey would be noticeably quicker due to the favourable winds and currents. Despite the enormous risks involved, Polynesians used this technique to find and chart almost every single habitable island in the South Pacific.

The principal navigational tools used by the Polynesians were the sun, moon, and stars, and as any visitor to the South Pacific will know, the clarity of the night skies in these parts is a marvel to behold. Understanding the position and trajectory of certain guide stars was a fundamental part of any Polynesian navigator's toolkit, and this specific knowledge was passed on to students at dedicated schools for celestial navigation. Sadly, very little of this information has survived, although stick charts (called *rebbelibs*) that display the connection between the islands and the major ocean swells that surround them, are still in use today in Micronesia and may have once been employed all across the Pacific. Before any long voyage, maps of the stars and of the expected currents would have to be learned by heart, as well as the predicted position of the sun and any other visible features along the way. In this way, the navigator was able to build up a mental picture of the necessary waypoints to follow, and this same technique would also form the basis for recording the location of new islands once they had been discovered.

Equally impressively, the Polynesians developed an extraordinary ability to sense the presence of land long before it was visible to the human eye. During the course of a sea passage, navigators would be constantly monitoring the atmospheric and oceanic conditions around them, since any noticeable convergence of swells could signify the presence of something in the water ahead, and possibly a new island just over the horizon. It is said that the master navigators were able to feel these tiny changes in the currents with their bodies, as opposed to necessarily seeing them with their eyes, and would temporarily relinquish their position at the helm of the canoe in order to lie down on the deck and feel its motion.

Cloud formations that developed around the canoe were also closely studied, together with the colour of the sky at both sunrise and sunset, since these features all contained possible clues regarding the presence of land nearby. As warm air from land rises up into the atmosphere, both the pressure and temperature of that air subsequently drop and form clouds, meaning that the appearance of certain cloud formations in the distance was potentially of enormous importance. Aside from clouds, any drifting land vegetation spotted in the sea would be a clear sign that land was close by, as was the unusual phenomenon of bioluminescence in the ocean, consisting of sharp flashes of light close to shore and visible from up to 150 miles away.

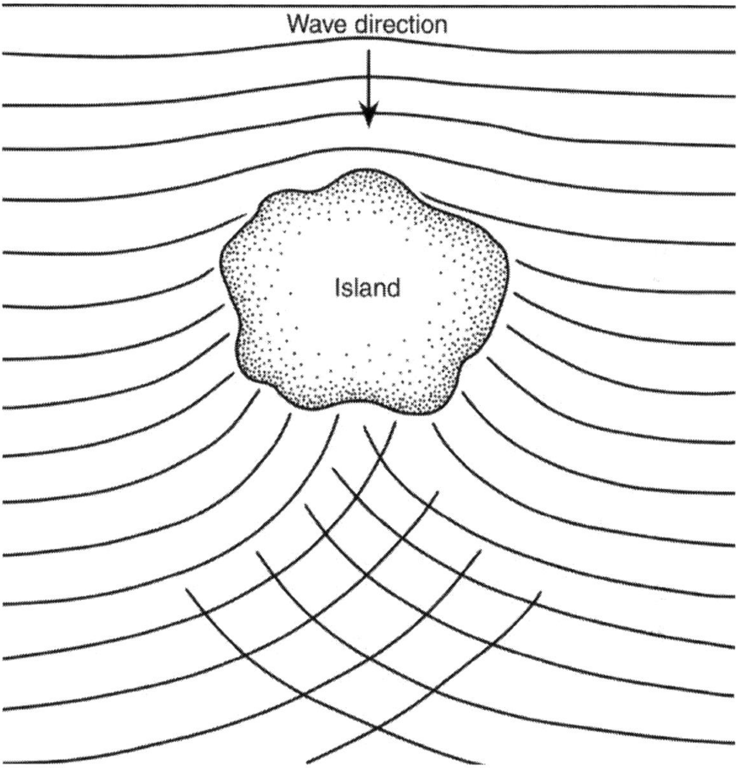

Within about a 50-mile radius of an island, the Polynesians would expect to start seeing seabirds around their canoes, and while some species can spend months at sea and only return to land in order to breed, diurnal seabirds feed on fish during the day and return to their nests each evening. Tracking the course of these birds as they flew out to their feeding grounds in the morning or returned to land late in the afternoon, gave navigators a good idea of the direction in which land may lie. Only during the nesting season does this behaviour change, when birds fly out to sea before sunrise and return to land by mid-morning in order to feed their young.

With the appearance of a new island hopefully imminent, those on board the canoe would now be scanning the horizon for the the first sign of land. There are numerous factors that dictate how close to an island you have to be before it becomes visible to the human eye, although fundamentally it depends on the height of the island, the climatic conditions at the time, and the position of the person looking out. Assuming that the Polynesians were making their observations from only a few feet above sea level, on a clear day they could probably have sighted a tall, mountainous island such as Tahiti (highest point: 7,352 feet) from over 80 miles away, whereas a low coral atoll such as Rangiroa (highest point: its tallest palm tree) would only have been visible from about 8 to 10 miles. For this reason, the Tuamotu Islands in French Polynesia, made up of a myriad of low-lying coral atolls and reefs, posed such a threat to early sailors and were more commonly referred to as the 'Dangerous Archipelago' or even the 'Labyrinth'.

The scouts generally planned to arrive at a new island in the early morning, as this provided them with the necessary visibility for navigating their way through reefs and any other hidden obstacles close to shore, as well as affording precious hours of daylight on land in order to explore their new surroundings. An island was assessed for its habitability, and particularly for the natural resources that it offered, including access to fresh water, availability of good fishing grounds, and the potential for farming land. The newly-arrived visitors took note of which animals and plants were already present, and subsequently drew up a list of those which would need to be introduced; with all of this information gathered and the island's exact location recorded, the scouts returned to their canoes and began the long journey back to their homeland. Once safely home, they reported their discoveries to the island's chiefs, and if it was agreed that this new land should be settled, several of the large ocean-going canoes would be prepared, each one capable of carrying up to 80 people together with large amounts of cargo.

Everything that was required for the settlement of the new island would have to be loaded on board, including various species of animals and plants, as well as a genetically viable human population. The plants that were carried were nearly all of the edible variety, such as yams, taro, bamboo, and coconut, while the introduced animals were generally always the same four species: pigs, dogs, chickens, and rats. The issue of whether Polynesians deliberately brought rats to new islands remains a point of discussion today, with some experts believing that they were specifically imported to provide a rapid source of protein, while others consider the rodents to have been nothing more than opportunistic stowaways whose dispersion all over the Pacific was an unfortunate consequence of these human migrations.

After retracing the same route previously sailed by the scouts, this sizeable group eventually arrived at their new island and began introducing the plants and animals that they had brought with them. The arrival of dogs, pigs, and chickens to islands where these species hadn't previously existed does not appear to have significantly affected the ecosystem of their new surroundings, and all three species continue to exist in healthy numbers on most Pacific Islands today. However, the introduction of Polynesian rats (*Rattus exulans*) has not been so positive, and the damaging effects of their arrival continue to be felt throughout the region. Capable of reproducing at an exponential rate, the rats soon overwhelmed large parts of the islands' ecosystems and caused irreversible damage to the native flora and seabird populations. The disappearance of swathes of ancient forest on both Hawai'i and Easter Island has also been blamed in part on the sizeable Polynesian rat population found on each island, and the taste that the rats acquired for the seeds of the native palm trees thus preventing them from germinating. Only after European visitors introduced the larger, more dominant Brown rat (*Rattus norvegicus*) to the Pacific from the 18th century onwards, did Polynesian rat numbers start to decline, and on some islands they have now disappeared completely.

Given the scale and success of the Polynesian expansion, the first European visitors to the region were greatly surprised not to find any uninhabited islands left for them to claim, noting with dismay that the Polynesians had always got there first! Prior to the arrival of the Europeans, many of the Pacific Islands had existed for up to 1,000 years without ever receiving a any non-Polynesian visitors, and relied entirely on neighbouring islands to obtain the necessary resources for their survival, everything from food supplies to enlarging the human gene pool. In extremely remote places such as Easter Island, the indigenous population may have lived in complete isolation for over 700 years without any outside visitors whatsoever, a testament to their deeply ingrained levels of autonomy and self-sufficiency.

Why?

Recent archaeological studies together with the Polynesians' own oral history have gone a long way to explaining how this remarkable migration unfolded, yet neither source tells us much about why it took place on such a large scale and over such a prolonged period of time. It can be explained on one level by the constant need for new land as populations on these small islands continued to grow, thus putting intense pressure on the limited resources. Since these islands were generally free of predators and diseases, they were extremely safe and pleasant places to live, and as such provided the ideal conditions for exponential population growth. However, as the Easter Island chapter later in this book will demonstrate, there is a fine line on small islands between a population size that is healthy and therefore thrives, and one that is unsustainably large for the available resources and consequently collapses.

Changes in the climatic conditions of these islands also played a crucial role in their habitability, and today we have a much better understanding of the detrimental effects of extreme weather, as well as the grave threat posed by rising sea levels to low-lying islands. Two climate patterns unique to the Pacific Ocean, known as El Niño and La Niña, occur about twice every decade and generally last for up to one year at a time, although this has been significantly longer recently. During an El Niño cycle, ocean temperatures rise and cause tropical fish species to abandon the region in search of cooler waters, while La Niña has the opposite effect, and the lower ocean temperatures can lead to droughts and more severe cyclones. The impact of these climatic patterns on the lives of the early Polynesians would have been as far-reaching as they were dramatic, and may well have forced islanders to look for new places to inhabit. Additionally, there were human factors that contributed to the displacement of people away from their original homes, and Polynesian oral histories are littered with tales of fierce wars between rivalling groups of warriors. In the case of battles that took place on the same island, it is highly probable that the losing faction would have been forced to leave and relocate elsewhere, resulting in an enforced voyage to a new land.

Finally, there is the deep-rooted human need to push boundaries and explore the outer limits of our world, and in this respect the Polynesians were no exception. As they sailed progressively further east, they would have had no idea just how far this watery world extended, or who or what awaited them at the end of it all. While their continuing discovery of islands that were uninhabited made the settlement process infinitely easier, it wasn't until they arrived at the west coast of South America that they met with their first non-Polynesian civilisations and could finally confirm that the world did in fact contain many more cultures than just their own.

Polynesia Today

Global geopolitics have rarely focused on the Pacific Ocean, and even the early European explorers who were visiting its many islands were actually in these waters searching for a different continent altogether. Nowadays, most people overfly Polynesia on direct flights between the U.S. and Australasia, unaware of the remarkable human history that took place on the ocean beneath them. If you are fortunate enough to traverse the region by ship, then idyllic sailing days with nothing but the sea to contemplate can offer a rare glimpse into the voyaging world of the ancient Polynesians.

From the 19th century onwards, many Pacific cultures suffered irreversible damages due to the arrival of outside visitors to the region, and the Polynesians were particularly affected by two significant events in their recent history. Religious missionaries from Europe and South America reached almost every island in Polynesia and successfully converted nearly all of them to Christianity, thus drastically changing the Polynesian belief systems as well as their cultural practices. Nevertheless, this attitude of the missionaries must be balanced with the fact they probably saved some island communities from certain extinction thanks to the western medicine that they introduced at the same time.

Subsequent visitors to the region stayed for a much shorter length of time, but their actions would have even more damaging consequences for those island communities. Slave traders, or blackbirders, arrived in Polynesia during the 19th century due to the sudden requirement for cheap labour after the abolition of slavery, leading to tens of thousands of Pacific Islanders being forcibly removed from their homelands and taken to work in unbearable conditions, mainly in South America. Many of the Pacific Islands were still independent nations at this time and were therefore defenceless to prevent these kidnappings from taking place. International protests eventually led to the outlawing of this barbaric practice, but not before some adult populations had been entirely decimated. A few of the survivors were eventually repatriated back to their native islands, but many introduced infectious diseases such as smallpox and measles, against which none of their fellow islanders had any natural defences.

The recent revival of Polynesian cultures throughout the world owes much to the efforts of the Polynesian Voyaging Society (PVS) in Hawai'i from the 1970s onwards, at a time when the region's languages and customs were often being either ignored or even repressed. With its principal aim of preserving the ancient art of celestial navigation, the PVS built a double-hulled voyaging canoe based on traditional designs and named it *Hokule'a*. In 1976, they made their inaugural sea passage from Hawai'i to Tahiti, navigating entirely by the sun and stars, and thus successfully completed the first long-distance, inter-island expedition undertaken by Polynesians for centuries. Ever since that historic voyage, the *Hokule'a* has continued to sail to every corner of Polynesia, and even circumnavigated the globe on a three-year voyage aimed at showcasing Polynesian culture and the urgent need to protect our oceans. Many other Pacific Islands have now built their own traditional canoes and have re-established navigation schools for young adults, where the next generations of Polynesian navigators are being taught the same skills that their ancestors employed so successfully. They follow in the sizeable footsteps of a group of intrepid explorers who settled one of the most inhospitable regions on Earth: the remote Pacific Ocean.

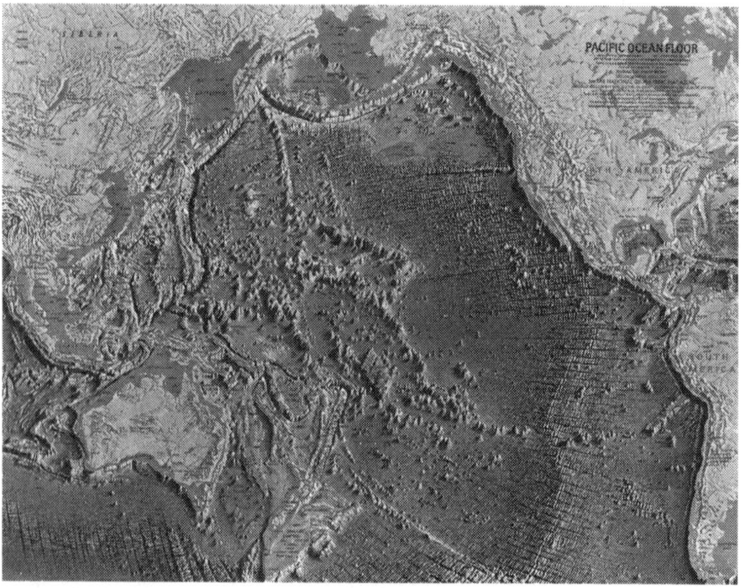

2. Captain Cook in the Pacific

'There is always the exceptional man, the man of independent mind and thought, who is ready to break away; and such a man was James Cook. Nothing less than the most efficient methods and procedures available would satisfy him, whether for marine surveying, charting or navigating. He was alive to all that was going on around him, and to all that was new in his profession.'

– Eva Taylor

Captain James Cook has long been regarded as one of the greatest explorers in maritime history, and our current understanding of early Polynesian culture owes much to his extensive travels in the region. During his three voyages to the Pacific Ocean, he succeeded in discovering the freezing boundaries of both the Arctic and Antarctica, and became the first outsider to set foot on many of the islands of Polynesia and beyond. Despite regularly finding himself in life-threatening situations – both from nature and from other humans – Cook still managed to make numerous pioneering discoveries that had a profound impact on 18th century scientific knowledge. His reputation in the Pacific today remains as robust as ever, and Cook's legacy has been preserved in the names of countless places and natural features throughout the entire region. For a man of humble, working-class origins, he enjoyed a meteoric rise in the Royal Navy and has since become one of the most celebrated Englishmen in history.

James Cook was born in the village of Marton, Yorkshire in 1728, the son of a farm labourer who had swapped his native Scotland for the northeast of England. Seeing that James was an intelligent and inquisitive young boy, his father's employer paid for his early education, something that was beyond the means of the Cook family given their eight children and meagre income.

On finishing school, James briefly worked as a shopkeeper in the coastal town of Whitby, and it was here that his fascination with the sea first took root. He accepted an apprenticeship with a local shipping company and set sail for the first time at the age of 18, working as a deckhand on a collier transporting coal to London.

Cook was a dedicated apprentice sailor, and despite his lack of formal education, he studied tirelessly in order to teach himself navigation, astronomy, and trigonometry. Most importantly, he learned how to draw accurate maps, a skill that he would later perfect during the course of his naval career. He spent the next nine years working on a variety of merchant ships around the British Isles, gaining valuable experience of sailing in challenging conditions, all of which resulted in him being offered the command of his own ship for the first time in 1755. However, despite the obvious economic benefits of such a position, he turned it down in favour of a more stable career in the Royal Navy, where he enlisted as an able seaman at the relatively 'experienced' age of 27.

Cook was soon promoted to the rank of Master's mate, and when the Seven Years' War with France broke out the following year, he saw action first in the English Channel and subsequently in Canada, where his cartography skills were credited for one of the British victories in Quebec. Within three years of enlisting, he had been promoted to Master, the most senior deck-working seaman on board a navy ship, and a remarkable rise given his lowly background and lack of influential connections. During the same period, he also married Elizabeth Batts, the daughter of one of his mentors, with whom he would go on to have six children.

The Royal Navy was a deeply classist and hierarchical institution at the time, with its commissioned officers nearly all hailing from aristocratic families, thus making any further promotion extremely unlikely for Cook. Nevertheless, in 1768 the 40-year-old James Cook was finally promoted to the rank of Lieutenant and offered the command of a ship that had only recently been acquired by the Royal Navy, named *The Earl of Pembroke.* Originally a collier, she was purchased especially for her inaugural voyage and rechristened HMS *Endeavour*, a name that would ultimately pass into the annals of British maritime history. Cook's first voyage coincided with the final years of the Age of Discovery, and the start of a period of scientific enlightenment in which the Pacific Ocean was still seen as a last frontier. The Royal Society of London, an influential group of academics and wealthy patrons, was actively promoting all fields of scientific advancement and petitioned King George III to finance an expedition to Tahiti in order to observe the Transit of Venus, an event which wouldn't repeat itself for another 105 years. The planet Venus was due to pass in-between the Earth and the Sun for about six hours on 3rd June 1769, and by measuring how long this crossing took from various parts of the world, it was thought possible to calculate the approximate size of the solar system.

Tahiti had only been discovered by Europeans the previous year, and first-hand accounts of a paradisiacal island and its amorous women had already found their way back to England. For this reason, it wasn't difficult to recruit sailors for this maiden voyage of the *Endeavour*, and the Royal Society even sent one of its most highly regarded young botanists, Joseph Banks, to accompany the expedition. The official purpose of the voyage was to observe and measure the Transit of Venus, but the Admiralty also handed Cook a further set of sealed instructions which he was to open only after he had completed his first mission. The *Endeavour* set sail from Plymouth Harbour in August 1768 and arrived in Tahiti in April of the following year, in plenty of time to witness the rare astronomical event under clear, cloudless skies. As a result of the crew's measurements, scientists were able to estimate that the distance between the Earth and the Sun was approximately 95,000,000 miles, with modern scientific techniques having proved that they were in fact only wrong by just over 2%!

Cook now opened his secret orders, and learned that he was to sail due south as far as Latitude 40° S and try to discover *Terra Australis Incognita*, the Unknown Southern Land. The Greek philosopher Aristotle had believed that a large continent must exist in the southern hemisphere in order to balance all of the land in the northern hemisphere, and despite there being no actual proof of its existence, it was included in all world maps from the 16th century onwards. The Royal Society also accepted Aristotle's theory and was keen that Britain should claim the Unknown Southern Land before any other rival power. Before sailing south, Cook and his crew explored the neighbouring islands of Huahine, Raiatea, Bora Bora, and Maupiti and claimed them all for Great Britain, naming the group the 'Society Islands'. In Raiatea they took a young Polynesian priest called Tupaia on board with them, who served as both a translator and local navigator. When the crew questioned him about the surrounding islands, they were astonished when he was able to draw a map of all 130 islands within a 2,000-mile radius of Raiatea.

From the Society Islands they continued south, performing an extensive search of the waters as far as 40° S in the hope that it would lead them to the edge of the Unknown Southern Land. However, after exploring over 1,500 miles of freezing ocean without discovering a single piece of dry land, they followed the Admiralty's subsequent instructions and headed west towards Australia. By October 1769 they had arrived at New Zealand, thus becoming only the second Europeans to sight it. The Māori had aggressively chased off the first visitors, led by the Dutch explorer Abel Tasman, before they had even had a chance to explore, and Cook's initial interactions with the Māori were no less hostile, resulting in several violent confrontations. The presence of Tupaia as an interpreter and mediator between the two parties proved to be of enormous benefit, and the Māori held him in high regard for his extensive cultural and geographical knowledge.

The *Endeavour* performed complete circumnavigations of both the North and South Islands of New Zealand, voyages which confirmed in Cook's mind that a Southern Land could not exist anywhere north of Latitude 40° S, at least not in the Pacific Ocean. Beneath that latitude he had no way of knowing for sure, but Cook had now completed his final instruction from the Admiralty and decided to set sail for home. He chose a westerly route back to England due to the difficulties of rounding Cape Horn during the austral winter, and so the *Endeavour* became the first European ship to visit the east coast of Australia, arriving at Botany Bay on 29th April 1770. Cook spent the next four months mapping the Australian coastline, which was crucial work for all future expeditions given the treacherous network of reefs scattered along the east coast. Unfortunately, disaster struck while they were sailing towards the northern tip of Queensland, and a navigational error caused the *Endeavour* to crash into the Great Barrier Reef at night. The crew were fortunate not to lose the ship completely, and they salvaged her by throwing six of the cannons and any other heavy objects overboard until she could finally be refloated, before inching their way cautiously towards the shore.

The party spent the next seven weeks on land, at a site known today as Cooktown, where they repaired the badly damaged *Endeavour* and tended to the sick, who by now included Tupaia. The crew had been badly affected by scurvy during this latest leg of the voyage, and Cook's studies into possible remedies for this poorly understood disease became invaluable for the Royal Navy, who subsequently shared the results across the entire fleet. He hadn't yet identified Vitamin C deficiency as the exact cause, but had been insisting that his men receive a fresh diet throughout the journey and had not lost a single one to scurvy so far, an extremely rare achievement for long-distance sailing in the 18th century. Without knowing exactly why, Cook had identified citrus fruit and sauerkraut, a traditional German dish of fermented raw cabbage, as excellent food sources for maintaining the health of his men, and when he had difficulties in convincing sailors to eat the latter, he famously made it a privileged item that was served only to the officers. As expected, the crew soon demanded that they also receive their fair share of this delicacy, to the extent that it eventually had to be rationed!

This lengthy stay in northern Australia also enabled Cook and his crew to enjoy regular interactions with the Aboriginal people, and while the indigenous inhabitants were initially extremely shy towards their European visitors, and then increasingly threatening, nevertheless Cook left Australia with a very positive opinion of them. From Australia the *Endeavour* crossed the Torres Strait to New Guinea, and within a few weeks they had arrived at the port of Batavia, present-day Jakarta, the then capital of the Dutch East Indies. The crew disembarked in high spirits and relatively good health after a long and eventful crossing of the Pacific Ocean, but were soon to suffer terribly from the lack of local sanitation, with severe outbreaks of malaria and dysentery particularly prevalent. While in Batavia, disease claimed the lives of a number of Cook's men, amongst them their loyal Polynesian companion, Tupaia.

The *Endeavour* made its way back to England via South Africa and Saint Helena and sailed up the English Channel in July 1771, nearly three years after her departure. Long voyages of this nature were considered so dangerous at the time that few people expected the *Endeavour* to return, and Cook's safe arrival was a cause for great celebration. Following the rules of the Royal Navy, the crew's journals and maps were all handed over to the Admiralty, and Cook was able to present them with the first detailed charts of the Society Islands, New Zealand, and the east coast of Australia. He was also able to confirm that much of the presumed Unknown Southern Land was, in fact, ocean. He was praised for having maintained such good health and tight discipline amongst the crew of the *Endeavour* and for his positive interactions with the native communities that they had encountered. In light of all of this, Cook was promoted to the rank of Commander shortly after his return.

Cook received much less positive news when he visited his family home in East London, where he was looking forward to rejoining his wife, Elizabeth, and their children, the fourth of whom had not yet been born when he'd sailed. Unfortunately, the boy Joseph had died at birth, and their daughter, Elizabeth, had also passed away a few months before Cook's return. His two eldest sons were growing up well, but it was a sad and seemingly short-lived homecoming, with a second expedition back to the Pacific very much in the Admiralty's plans.

Within months of his return, Cook had been asked to find two suitable ships for a return voyage to the South Seas that he would again command. Wary of the near disaster that had befallen the *Endeavour* at the Great Barrier Reef, Cook insisted that they sail with two ships this time, and thus avoid the risk of becoming completely stranded in the event of an accident. He selected two vessels for the Navy to buy and oversaw the completion of all the necessary modifications for another prolonged global voyage. In the meantime, the botanist Joseph Banks had become something of a celebrity in England due to his discoveries in the South Pacific and had even proposed that he should lead the next expedition himself, with Cook serving beneath him. Fortunately for Cook, Banks didn't approve of the ships that had been purchased for this second voyage, and he somewhat haughtily refused to sail with them. Banks would later be elected President of the Royal Society at the age of just 35, a post which he held for the next 41 years, and he would also be the driving force behind the creation of Kew Gardens in London.

In July 1772, less than a year after the completion of Cook's first circumnavigation of the world, HMS *Resolution* and HMS *Adventure* set sail from Plymouth Harbour, bound for the Pacific. Cook captained the *Resolution* and had overall command of the expedition, while the *Adventure* was led by Tobias Furneaux, who had served as a Second Lieutenant on HMS *Dolphin* in 1767 and had been the first European to ever set foot on Tahiti. Their orders for this second voyage were to confirm the existence of the Unknown Southern Land once and for all, by venturing further south than anyone had ever sailed before, and to test the Navy's new K1 marine chronometer, designed to help better calculate longitude.

While in the Indian Ocean somewhere between Africa and Australia, the two ships sailed beneath the Antarctic Circle for the first time, reaching as far south as 67° S, but they discovered no landmass or islands, only endless icebergs. At one point the *Resolution* was within 50 miles of the edge of the Antarctic continent, but with conditions becoming increasingly unpleasant and limited cold-weather clothing for the crew, they were forced to retreat north. Soon afterwards, the two ships lost sight of each other in the dense Antarctic fog, and both made their way independently to Queen Charlotte Sound in New Zealand, where they had arranged to rendezvous in the event of becoming separated.

During their time apart, the *Adventure* charted modern-day Tasmania, while Cook and the *Resolution* revisited the South Island of New Zealand, before successfully reuniting with each other three months later. Cook was dismayed to learn of numerous cases of scurvy amongst the crew of the *Adventure*, as well as an outbreak of venereal disease, which the men were unashamedly passing on to the Māori womenfolk. Once discipline had been restored on board, the two ships continued together from New Zealand into the South Pacific, basing themselves in Tahiti after the excellent relations that had been established between the British and the Tahitians during the visit of the *Endeavour*. The expedition's artist, William Hodges, was sailing on board the *Resolution*, and some of his watercolours from this voyage provide a rare insight into everyday life in 18th century Polynesia. Interestingly, the landscapes for which Hodges is now so famous were only lightly sketched while he was in the Pacific, with the full oil paintings not completed until he was back in England.

The two ships spent the winter months exploring the Society and Tuamotu Groups, before making their way back towards New Zealand via the islands of Tonga. After the success of having had Tupaia accompany them during the voyage of the *Endeavour*, Cook allowed a Tahitian stowaway called Mai to remain on board the *Adventure* when he was discovered soon after their departure from the Society Islands. Unlike Tupaia however, Mai was neither a priest nor an expert navigator, but he demonstrated a keen enthusiasm to sail with the British, and if possible, to accompany them all the way back to England.

The Tongans welcomed their new visitors effusively, generously exchanging goods with them and organising extravagant Polynesian dance performances for them each evening. This lavish hospitality led Cook to christen Tonga 'The Friendly Isles', which was ultimately a complete misnomer – the Tongans were in fact planning to lure the British into a false sense of security before killing them and stealing their ships. Fortunately for Cook and his crew, the plan stalled when the Tongans were unable to decide whether to attack during the day or at night, and when relations with the locals began to deteriorate anyway, Cook suddenly chose to weigh anchor and leave for New Zealand instead. Somewhat ironically, the Tongan Tourism Board continues to this day to promote their islands using the name given to them by Cook, with most visitors blissfully unaware about the actual circumstances surrounding 'The Friendly Isles'!

While approaching New Zealand, The *Adventure* and the *Resolution* again became separated from each other during a fierce storm, and both crews reasoned that they would rendezvous in Queen Charlotte Sound as before. Independently of each other, the men of both ships would now be spending much more time in New Zealand than they had ever intended, and be introduced to a much more gruesome side of Māori culture. While rumours concerning cannibalism in the Pacific Islands had been widely shared amongst the early European explorers, few had ever witnessed it first-hand, and many of Cook's men, including Mai, were appalled by what they saw in New Zealand. The Māori goaded the British as they feasted upon the entrails of defeated victims, seemingly relishing their visitors' disgust at their behaviour.

This time, however, the planned reuniting of the two ships never took place, and the *Resolution* and the *Adventure* would never see each other again on this voyage. The *Resolution* had arrived earlier than her sister ship and spent an entire month waiting at Ship Cove, before Cook became impatient and decided to return to sea and renew his search for the Unknown Southern Land. The *Adventure* arrived at Queen Charlotte Sound just four days later, and discovered a message that Cook had left in a bottle on the beach, advising the crew of his plans. On 17th December 1773, Furneaux ordered a group of men from the *Adventure* to row ashore and stock up on fresh food in preparation for their long voyage ahead, while also insisting that they be back on board by mid-afternoon. When the men hadn't returned by nightfall, a rescue party was sent ashore at first light the following morning, where they discovered pieces of the rowboat and a crewmember's shoe, and much more disconcertingly, pieces of fresh meat which they desperately hoped had once belonged to an animal. Only when they found a human hand with the unmistakable tattoo of one of their companions, did they realise exactly what had occurred the previous day, namely that all ten men had been brutally murdered and disembowelled. The *Adventure* set sail the very same day, but the crew never renewed their search for *Terra Australis Incognita* and instead sailed straight back to England via Cape Horn, utterly traumatised by their experience at Grass Cove.

Cook and the *Resolution* spent the next 12 months at sea, sailing down into the Antarctic region and visiting new islands in the Pacific such as the Marquesas, Easter Island, and Fiji. They survived violent storms, freezing temperatures, and illnesses that severely affected most of the crew, including Cook himself. On two separate occasions they again sailed beneath the Antarctic Circle, at one point reaching 71°10' S, the furthest south that anyone had ever been at that time, and they were only prevented from venturing even further by solid sea ice. When Cook was finally ready to leave the region, after yet another return to New Zealand and a final run across the Pacific Ocean to Cape Horn, he was absolutely convinced that *Terra Australis Incognita* did not exist, but that a small polar continent probably did, and that they had just found the very edge of it.

The *Resolution* arrived back in Portsmouth in July 1775, over three years after her departure, and Cook's latest expedition was again considered to have been a resounding success; the existence of the Unknown Southern Land had effectively been disproven, and the K1 chronometer had maintained near-perfect accuracy throughout the voyage, allowing for a much more precise calculation of their longitudinal position. Cook's charts of the South Pacific were gratefully received by the Admiralty and they were considered so accurate that they remained in use until as recently as the Second World War. Cook was promoted to the rank of Captain and was awarded his honourable retirement from the Royal Navy, despite his insistence that he be reinstated immediately if a suitable voyage ever arose.

That voyage arrived sooner than he might have imagined, and it came in the form of someone who had reached England on the *Adventure* the previous year and who Cook may well have forgotten about completely, namely Mai. The young Polynesian had become something of a celebrity in the upper echelons of British society, and had even enjoyed several audiences with King George III himself. However, despite his novelty value in England, the Admiralty recognised that they had a duty to return him to his homeland, and so another voyage to the South Pacific was proposed for the following year.

In reality, the motive for this expedition wasn't solely a humanitarian one; the Royal Society was anxious for Britain to be first to discover the fabled Northwest Passage, believed to link the Pacific and Atlantic Oceans across the top of North America. The expedition was to be commanded by Charles Clerke, with Cook initially hired as a consultant; however, his undeniable experience soon shone through and convinced the Admiralty that the voyage should in fact be led by their most accomplished captain once more. Cook was given the command of HMS *Resolution* for a second time, while Clerke captained the smaller HMS *Discovery*, having sailed with Cook on both of his previous Pacific voyages. The *Resolution*'s Master, the person responsible for the ship's navigation, was a recently promoted young officer by the name of William Bligh, who would find fame for all the wrong reasons 13 years later while in command of HMS *Bounty*.

Captain Cook's retirement had lasted for less than a year, and the *Resolution* left Plymouth Harbour on 12th July 1776, with the *Discovery* following soon after. The two ships met up in Cape Town and from there sailed together to New Zealand, returning to Cook's favourite anchorage at Queen Charlotte Sound. It was a tense reunion with the local Māori, who were convinced that Cook had come back to seek revenge for the atrocities committed against the crew of the *Adventure* three years earlier, and many of the men aboard his own ships were also expecting him to exact some form of retribution. When he did nothing, some of the crew saw this as a weakness in his leadership, and for the first time during any of his extensive voyages, Cook's authority began to be questioned.

From New Zealand they sailed to Cook's other favourite anchorage in the Pacific, Matavai Bay in Tahiti, where they stocked up with supplies in preparation for the long voyage ahead. Mai was finally returned to his homeland, and the crew even built him a European-style house and decorated it with western furniture. Cook was unusually emotional at having to bid farewell to their young companion, but he also later acknowledged in his journal that he thought the two-year stay in England had had little effect on Mai, and that the social experiment had been of scant benefit to either the British or the Tahitians. They sailed due north from Tahiti and became the first Europeans to visit the Hawaiian Islands, where they were surprised to discover a thriving Polynesian society in spite of the isolation. Both ships then continued north and spent the following six months exploring the Pacific coastline of North America and rounding the Alaskan peninsula, which Cook managed to demonstrate was not in fact an island as previous maps of the area had suggested. They passed through the Bering Strait, separating Russia and Alaska, before turning east and somewhat optimistically expecting that they would be able to sail from there directly into the Atlantic. It wasn't the case, and by August 1778 they had been prevented from continuing any further by impenetrable sea ice and were forced to turn around. They had made some significant discoveries along the way, including reaching as far north as 70°44' N and charting all of the waters as far west as Siberia, before returning through the Bering Strait and sailing back towards Hawai'i.

The exact events surrounding Cook's second visit to the Hawaiian Islands are unclear, but we do know that he arrived in low spirits and possibly poor health after many months spent in the frigid waters of the Arctic. As if by fate, the arrival of the British coincided with the start of the local festival of Makahiki, organised each year to honour the Hawaiian god of fertility and abundance, Lono. The Hawaiians regarded Cook's timely arrival as evidence that he was the embodiment of Lono himself, and the British were given a lavish welcome by the islanders and inundated with gifts.

In early February 1779, after several months of generous hospitality from the Hawaiians, the crew reluctantly prepared the *Resolution* and the *Discovery* for their journey back to the Arctic Circle and set sail northwards once again. Not long after their departure, a violent storm damaged the mast of the *Resolution*, and Cook decided to turn back to Hawai'i for repairs, returning to their previous anchorage at Kealakekua

Bay on the Big Island. However, this time the British were not welcomed warmly, since the period of the Makahiki festival had now finished, and Lono was not expected to return so soon. The Hawaiians were now belligerent and unfriendly, and a large, threatening crowd began to gather on the shore and in the waters surrounding the two ships. Shortly afterwards, one of the rowing boats from the *Resolution* was stolen, and Cook took the unusual step of going ashore himself to try to negotiate its return, thus putting himself in imminent danger in the middle of an unruly throng. He had planned to lure a Hawaiian chief onto the *Resolution* and to keep him hostage until the skiff was returned, a ploy that had worked before on other islands in Polynesia, but on this occasion the crowd quickly realised what the British were intending to do. Several of the islanders set upon Cook, first striking him over the head with a club and then swiftly stabbing him in the neck, killing him instantly. He was 50 years old and less than a year away from completing the last of his remarkable Pacific voyages.

Despite the violent nature of his death, Cook was so revered by the Hawaiians that they organised an elaborate Polynesian funeral for him, a gesture usually only reserved for Hawaiian royalty. Some of his remains were eventually returned back to the crew of the *Resolution*, who also gave him a formal burial at sea with full military honours. It was an ignominious ending for possibly the Pacific's greatest explorer, and there was a profound sense of grief on board both of the ships at the loss of their captain and friend. Far beyond his achievements in all matters related to the sea, he was fondly remembered as 'an honest, caring and loyal leader of men, with a good instinct for danger and a strong sense for an imminent shoreline'.

Cook's third Pacific voyage was completed without its illustrious captain, and equally without ever discovering the Northwest Passage, an honour that would go to the Irish explorer Robert McClure 70 years later. The crews of the *Resolution* and the *Discovery* made one final attempt to locate the elusive passageway after leaving Hawai'i but eventually gave up and returned to England, where they arrived back to a subdued welcome in October 1780.

Elizabeth Cook lived for over 50 years after James' death, although none of their six children lived long enough to have any offspring of their own, meaning that there are no direct descendants of James and Elizabeth Cook today. However, the legacy of Britain's greatest maritime explorer remains alive and well in his beloved Pacific Ocean, and our understanding of these islands and of the people who once inhabited them, has been immeasurably enriched by the dedicated service of this humble sailor from Marton in Yorkshire.

3. The Real Robinson Crusoe: Alexander Selkirk

'I am monarch of all I survey;
My right there is none to dispute;
From the centre all round to the sea
I am lord of the fowl and the brute.
O Solitude! where are the charms
That sages have seen in thy face?
Better dwell in the midst of alarms,
Than reign in this horrible place.'

– William Cowper, The Solitude of Alexander Selkirk (1782)

The question of whether you could survive by yourself on a desert island is one that many of us ask ourselves at some point, even if very few people are ever presented with the opportunity for such extreme solitude. Those who do find themselves in this rare predicament are usually the victims of accidents or shipwrecks, and only a very small number of them ever survive to tell the tale. The hero of this chapter is particularly unusual, not only for the extraordinary adventure that he lived for four and a half years, but because he actually requested to be marooned on his uninhabited island in the first place.

Alexander Selcraig was born in 1676 in the Scottish fishing village of Lower Largo, on the northern edge of the Firth of Forth. He was the son of a local shoemaker and showed signs of a rebellious personality from an early age, despite being the youngest of seven brothers which in those days was considered to be a lucky omen. While little is known about his childhood, records show that at the age of 16 he was summoned to the disciplinary committee of his local parish council, accused of '*undecent beaiviar in ye church*', although the exact details of his misdemeanour fortunately remain unknown.

Despite the hopes of his father that he would one day follow him into the family business of leather tanning and shoemaking, Alexander instead felt drawn to a life of travel and adventure, and when he failed to appear for his hearing in front of the church council, it transpired that he'd run away from home the previous day and had fled to sea. During the 17th century, Largo Harbour was a popular port of call for British warships and merchant navy vessels, where they also recruited local men for crewing positions. It appears that the young Alexander had escaped on board one of these ships, joining an expedition to Central America that offered the promise of bountiful riches as well as a change from the drudgery of village life. However, the dream of undiscovered wealth in distant lands sadly never materialised, and a disillusioned Selcraig returned to his home in Scotland eight years later having barely survived the ordeal and still as poor as the day he left.

After enduring such a gruelling voyage during which many of his fellow crewmembers had succumbed to tropical diseases and starvation, it seems that Alexander's mischievous personality in childhood had now transformed into an aggressive one in adulthood. When one of his brothers left a tin of saltwater lying about their house and Alexander unwittingly drank from it, becoming the butt of his brother's jokes caused him to fly into a violent rage. He ended up assaulting almost every member of his family, including trying to shoot his brother with their father's pistol, and even attacked his own sister-in-law who had tried to separate the feuding brothers. For the second time in his life, he was summoned before the church elders to be '*rebuked in face of the congregation for his scandalous carriage*' and to explain his violent behaviour. This time he was present for his court hearing, where he admitted to his crimes and promised to improve his future conduct. A public shaming of this kind seemingly brought an end to the possibility of Alexander Selcraig remaining in Scotland with his family, and the call to a life on the high seas beckoned once more.

While there is no record of his recruitment or of how exactly he found his way on board, in 1703 the English sailing ship *Cinque Ports* listed its Master, and therefore the person tasked with the ship's navigation, as one **Alexander Selkirk**. In those days it was fairly common for people to sign up for ships under a pseudonym, although it was usually in circumstances when someone was trying to escape from either justice or from their past; in this instance it appears that Selcraig's surname was written with this particular spelling as an anglicisation of his Scottish family name. However, the *Cinque Ports* that he joined, whose own name paid homage to the confederation of five ports on the south coast of England, was neither a Royal Navy ship, nor even a merchant navy vessel; the *Cinque Ports* was, in fact, a pirate ship.

During the 17th and 18th centuries, 'privateering' was the elegant term for piracy with permission, when crews of sailors were authorised to criss-cross the world's oceans and commit robbery, kidnap, and even murder, all in the name of their governments. With the outbreak of the War of the Spanish Succession in 1701, England and Spain were effectively at continuous war with each other, and English privateers were tasked with causing as much damage as possible to Spanish interests around the world. Under the command of Captain Charles Pickering, the *Cinque Ports* was one such ship authorised for this purpose, and it was to sail together with the *St George* under its captain and expedition leader, William Dampier. Their original instructions had been to patrol the South Atlantic and attack Spanish galleons as they left Argentina with their bounties of gold, but this venture seems to have proved unsuccessful since they later altered their plans and continued sailing south towards Cape Horn.

An outbreak of scurvy on board while in the waters off Brazil had resulted in the deaths of many of the crew of the *Cinque Ports*, including the ship's popular captain, Charles Pickering. He was replaced by the 21-year-old Lieutenant Thomas Stradling, a far less popular choice by all accounts, but under Stradling's leadership and Selkirk's navigation, they successfully brought their ship around the Horn and into the Pacific Ocean. They sailed up the west coast of South America as far as Panama, but had limited success in capturing any enemy ships; they did manage to lay siege to one Spanish vessel, but its cargo contained neither gold nor any other valuable goods, and sensing it was too big a task for his reduced crew to manage two ships, Dampier chose not to appropriate it. They managed to capture one more ship during the next three months, but this did little to raise the spirits of the men, particularly when Dampier and Stradling kept most of the booty for themselves and refused to share it out evenly amongst the crew.

After nine challenging months at sea, the privateers had seen little in the way of action, and more importantly, had earned almost no money whatsoever, thus calling into question the purpose of the entire voyage. Privateers weren't paid a salary, but instead kept a percentage of the riches that they acquired during the expedition, meaning that in this case the men were facing the real possibility of returning home empty-handed. With both ships now running dangerously low on supplies and the crews in desperate need of food and rest, Dampier took the decision to call in at a small group of islands that had been discovered by the Spanish explorer Juan Fernández in 1574 and named in his honour. Located in the South Pacific over 400 miles from the Chilean coast, the islands offered an abundance of wild fruit and animals with which to replenish their food stocks, and would give the crew a much-needed opportunity to rest and recover.

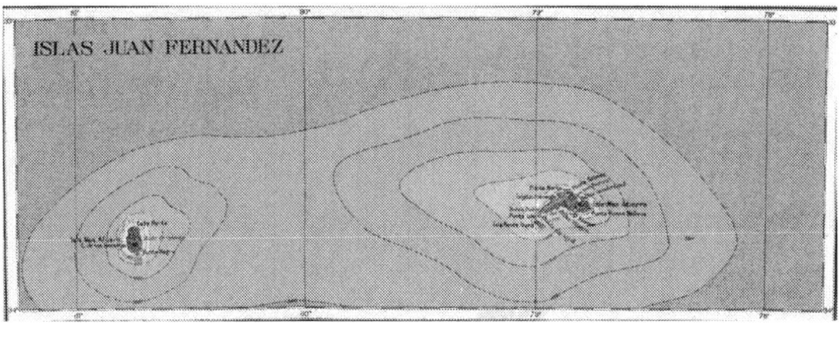

The Juan Fernández Archipelago consists of a series of small, uninhabited volcanic islands, the main two of which had been christened with possibly the least original names imaginable: the closest one to the South American mainland was *Isla Más Atierra* (Closer to Land Island), while the further of the two was *Isla Más Afuera* (Further from Land Island)! Dampier ordered the two ships to anchor off *Isla Más Atierra*, where the *Cinque Ports* arrived in September of 1704. By now its initial crew of 90 had been reduced to less than half of that number, and the remaining men were in poor physical condition, hungry, and frustrated with their captains. Selkirk in particular was unhappy with Stradling's treatment of the crew, and an air of mutinous discontent began to pervade the ship's decks. Ever since Panama, many of the men had been unimpressed by the strategies employed by the two captains, and felt that they should have been more aggressive with their tactics for apprehending enemy ships.

The two ships dropped anchor off *Isla Más Atierra* and the crews rowed ashore, where they were greeted by crowds of raucous fur seals basking on the beach, immediately providing the sailors with much-needed fresh meat and blubber. Some of the men headed into the interior of the island where they shot wild goats, while others fished in the abundant waters surrounding the island. During the month that the *Cinque Ports* spent there, the men gratefully took the opportunity to renew their spirits and regain their physical health, knowing that they would soon have to return to the high seas and resume their search for treasure.

Nevertheless, there was one pressing issue that could not be overlooked, and one that as the ship's Master, Selkirk himself was particularly aware of. Ever since they had departed from Panama, gradually widening gaps in the hull had meant that two men were forced to remain in the bowels of the ship at all times and pump out the water, and Selkirk realised that their chances of continuing on their voyage, let alone of returning to Britain alive at the end of it, were looking increasingly slim. The two ships had called in briefly at the Juan Fernández archipelago six months earlier and had left behind a cache of spare equipment for future repairs, only to discover when they arrived this time that the additional rigging, anchors, and masts had all been stolen. The crew did their best to carry out repairs on both ships with the limited materials available, but Selkirk considered the oak timbers of the *Cinque Ports* now to be completely rotten, and that it would be extremely foolish to return to the open ocean in such a leaky ship. Naval shipworm had by now penetrated much of the hull, and Selkirk recognised that significant structural repairs would be necessary in order to replace the ship's timbers and make the *Cinque Ports* seaworthy again. Stradling, the ship's inexperienced captain, had other ideas and was in a hurry to set sail. The men had generally recovered from their illnesses, food stocks had been replenished, and the ship sufficiently patched up to get them back out into the hunting grounds off Panama, where he believed they could easily capture another ship and use it for the remainder of their journey. He was keen to start building his personal fortune, and also eager to get back to England – he hadn't come all this way to spend months on a remote island in the South Pacific.

In early October, Stradling gave the order to weigh anchor and set sail for South America. Selkirk disagreed, and confident that he had the backing of the rest of the crew, he refused to obey his captain's orders and insisted that the ship would go nowhere but to the bottom of the ocean if she returned to sea at that moment. A bitter argument broke out between the two men, with Stradling accusing Selkirk of attempting to incite a mutiny, while Selkirk's own violent temper no doubt resurfaced once again. Aware that he was the ship's principal navigator, Selkirk threatened to remain on shore if further repairs were not carried out, and he tried desperately to convince others to join him in his standoff. Somewhat surprisingly, none of the other men did, and Selkirk quickly became an isolated figure amongst the crew, only for things to soon get a great deal lonelier for him. Stradling urgently needed to maintain his authority over his men and could not be seen to be giving in to a subordinate in public, and so informed Selkirk that he would be staying on the island after all, and that this was the least that he deserved for his insubordination. He ordered all of Selkirk's belongings to be offloaded from the ship, and when the now desperate Scotsman offered his apologies and begged to be allowed to remain with the crew, his pleas fell on deaf ears. His volatile temperament had cost him once again, but rather than a slap on the wrist from the church elders of Lower Largo, this time it was potentially going to cost him his life.

As Selkirk sat alone on the beach at *Isla Más Atierra* that evening, having watched his companions row back to their ship, weigh anchor, and gradually disappear over the horizon, one wonders what thoughts were going through his head at the time. He probably suspected that Stradling would ultimately take pity on him, and having given him a good scare, would turn the ship around and come back to collect him. Only when the *Cinque Ports* failed to return during the whole of the next day, did it finally dawn on Selkirk that his predicament was in fact real, and that he really had been cast away by his captain.

The Castaway

By all accounts the first few weeks of Alexander Selkirk's life as a castaway were exceedingly difficult, overwhelmed by a sense of anger towards his captain and crew for having abandoned him and equally angry at himself for having allowed his temper to get the better of him once again. Unable to rest and feeling constantly threatened by the wild animals on the island, he was exhausted, lonely, and terrified. Stradling had left him with the bare minimum of supplies: his clothing, some bedding, a musket together with a small amount of gunpowder, a knife, cooking pot, his navigational instruments, and a Bible. Selkirk had also kept some tobacco with him and a small bottle of rum, but neither lasted long under the duress of those first few weeks of solitude. Using his gun, he was able to kill the occasional feral goat and make fresh stew for himself, but lamented not having any spices with which to improve the flavour. He had used the flint from his gun to light his first fire, but with a limited supply of gunpowder he soon realised the importance of not ever allowing the fire to go out.

After several weeks of doing little more than gazing at the horizon and waiting patiently, Selkirk realised that he must abandon any hope of the *Cinque Ports* returning for him, or of being rescued by another passing ship; he wasn't listed as a missing person anywhere, and only Stradling and his crew knew that he was marooned. He contemplated building a raft and trying to sail away, but from his background as a navigator he knew that there was no other land nearby, and that he was at least 400 miles from the Chilean mainland. He would have been well aware of the strong current that flows parallel to South America, known today as the Humboldt current but as yet unchristened in 1704, and the fact that this would only carry him even further into the Pacific and away from where possible salvation might lie.

If escape from the island was impossible, he considered the option of taking his own life, since the human skulls that he discovered during his exploratory walks around the island were stark reminders that not all of those who arrived on this solitary outpost necessarily left it alive. While still on the *Cinque Ports*, he had witnessed a sailor's corpse being thrown overboard and his remains being fervently devoured by sharks, and so knew that certain death lay in the surrounding waters if he chose it. By now Selkirk was in poor mental and physical health, and his limited diet had left him with debilitating stomach issues, made worse by the fact that the few goats that he was able to shoot with his musket would often escape and die in inaccessible crannies within the mountains. To add insult to injury, it was spring in the southern hemisphere and the male fur seals were aggressively staking claim to their territories and to their mating partners, and poor Selkirk was considered to be a potential threat by them too, despite his lack of fur (yet!). Contrary to their docile image, male Juan Fernández fur seals can weigh up to 300 lbs, are capable of fighting each other to the death, and will bark and howl incessantly in order to scare away any potential challengers to their harem. With rescue and escape now both out of the question, Selkirk decided that it was time to withdraw from the chaos of the coastline, and search for some peace and quiet amongst the higher ground.

Selkirk settled on top of the mountain that overlooked the island's main bay and built himself two separate wooden cabins with sandalwood thatch: one as a kitchen and larder to store his very limited supplies and the other as a bedroom and place to read. He remembered something of his father's trade and cleaned up several goats' hides, which he then sewed together and hung from the walls of each hut to give him some protection from the elements. Selkirk still anticipated that he would soon be rescued, and so established a daily routine of visiting a lookout on a nearby mountain ridge every morning and evening, from where he optimistically scanned the surrounding ocean for any passing ships. Exploring more of the island, Selkirk managed to scavenge many of the tools, weapons, and furniture that he needed, and his diet also became progressively more varied. He learned how to kill even the most aggressive fur seals (you approach them from behind and stand alongside their bodies so that neither their teeth nor their tail can get you, apparently) and supplemented his diet with fish, lobster, wild berries, and seabirds' eggs. During this period, Selkirk seems to have been in a much more positive state of mind, feeling more at ease on his new island and less threatened by the elements and the animals with which he was sharing it. However, one species that continued to bother him on the high ground were the rats, which had previously been introduced to the island and had now become fearless in their pursuit of food. They devoured many of the supplies that Selkirk had stored in his larder and kept him awake at night by nibbling on his clothing and even at his toes! The solution to this problem came in the form of another introduced species, namely feral cats. He slowly coaxed them towards his huts using goat meat, and where possible he would steal their newborn kittens in order to domesticate them. The scent of his new companions was usually enough to keep the rats away, and he was finally able to store his food untouched and also to sleep peacefully at night.

Selkirk also domesticated newborn goats by breaking their hind legs so they were unable to stray far from him, and by the time that their limbs had healed, the animals were well accustomed to his presence. It was of little consequence to Selkirk when his gunpowder and ammunition finally ran out, as he had become so quick and agile by this point that he was able to catch wild goats with nothing but his bare hands. When his clothing eventually wore out, he again relied on the memory of his father's trade to sew himself a tunic from goats' hides; however, when he exhausted his only pair of shoes, he chose not to replace them, but rather to continue walking barefoot - the soles of his feet had by now become so hard from running across the island's volcanic terrain that he no longer required any footwear.

Within a year of his arrival, Selkirk had adapted to his new environment and had also succeeded in guaranteeing his long-term survival: he had a safe place to live, enjoyed a varied supply of food with which to sustain himself, and he had discovered various sources of freshwater from which to collect drinking water. Barring any unforeseen accidents and the unpleasant prospect of a slow and solitary death as a result, he felt reassured in the knowledge that he could continue to live in this way for as long as was necessary, and until such time as a passing ship eventually rescued him. However, even that occurrence wasn't necessarily straightforward, since it depended entirely on the nationality of the ship as to whether its crew would welcome him on board as a hero or kill him on the spot. England was still involved in a bitter war with Spain, and even as a Scotsman, Selkirk would be regarded as the sworn enemy if he was discovered by the Spanish. He decided that it would be preferable to stay on the island indefinitely rather than be captured by Spaniards, who would either murder him or otherwise lock him away in a brutal prison somewhere on the South American mainland.

On two occasions he experienced the elation of spotting a nearby ship from his mountain lookout, only for his excitement to quickly turn to terror each time once he identified the ships as Spanish. In both cases the crew called in at the island, although the first visitors never suspected that it was inhabited and so killed a few seals for their meat stores and left soon after. However, the second group remained ashore and explored much of the island on foot, and once they saw Selkirk's huts and well-tended garden, they correctly guessed that there was a local population. After catching a glimpse of the fleeing Scotsman in the distance they gave chase, at one point even relieving themselves beneath the very same tree whose branches Selkirk was hiding in. When the visitors eventually grew tired of searching for him, they restocked their ship with most of Selkirk's food stores and left the island for good.

These incidents of possible rescue followed by desperate flight took place just twice in over four years, and otherwise Selkirk had to continually face his only other real challenge: boredom. When he had been unceremoniously dumped on the island with only a few possessions to his name, the one book included with his belongings had been a copy of the King James Bible. Never a religious man during his days as a sailor, it appears that during his life as a castaway he did find some form of spiritual solace, and he would read passages from the Bible out loud in order to preserve the use of his voice. He even took to praying each evening, with the content of those prayers presumably dominated by the request for a passing English ship! He seems to have spent a great deal of time reminiscing about his days as a young man in Lower Largo, and made the promise to himself, and possibly to God too, that if he were ever to escape from this predicament, he would live out the rest of his days in a very different manner.

The irony of his situation was not lost on Selkirk: he had left the relative comfort of family life in Scotland to sail to the other side of the world in search of riches and glory and had ultimately ended up alone and penniless on a deserted island. And yet he appears to have discovered a certain degree of serenity which had eluded him during his privateering days and an acceptance that his destiny was completely out of his own hands. Having not seen an English ship for over four years, his overriding fear was that Spain may have already won the war by now, and that there would be only Spanish ships sailing in these waters for the foreseeable future.

Rescue

In September 1708 two English privateering ships, the *Duke* and the *Duchess*, set sail for the South Pacific under the command of Captain Woodes Rogers. Lacking skilled sailors (most of the crew were opportunists with limited sailing experience, looking simply to get rich quickly), they invited a retired ship's captain to sail with them in a consulting role, and in particular as a *'pilot for the South Seas'*. He was none other than William Dampier, commander of the same expedition that had abandoned Selkirk on *Isla Más Atierra* four years earlier, even if that particular decision had been taken by the accompanying ship's captain, Thomas Stradling. Despite the *Duke* and *Duchess* being sturdier and more seaworthy ships than the *St George* and the *Cinque Ports*, their voyage was an equally challenging one, beset by outbreaks of scurvy and drunkenness for the duration of the sea passage, and even murmurs of mutiny. With no notable conquests of enemy ships to raise the men's spirits, Dampier once again suggested that they put in at the Juan Fernández islands in order to replenish the ships' supplies and allow the men to recover.

Selkirk estimated that it was late January 1709 when he caught sight of two ships on the horizon, and by now he had been alone on his island home for nearly four and a half years. Recognising them almost immediately as English ships, he hurried down to the shoreline and lit an enormous fire, desperate not to let the ships pass him by. Ironically, the English interpreted this gesture as an aggressive act, and fearing that the island was inhabited by a Spanish garrison, they maintained a safe distance from the shore and sailed on. Convinced that his chance of rescue had vanished, an inconsolable Selkirk spent another night alone in his wooden hut, unaware that it was, in fact, to be the last time that he ever slept there.

The following morning, Selkirk was ecstatic to discover that the English had in fact anchored on the other side of the island, and this time he signalled to them by waving a simple white flag. The gesture worked, and by mid-morning the English ships had returned to the island's main bay where they cautiously approached the beach in their rowing boats. Terrified by the appearance of the man that greeted them, *'cloth'd in goat skins who look'd wilder than the first owners of them'*, the visitors swiftly tried to determine the identity of this unexpected inhabitant. With guns pointed at his chest, and unable to speak due to fear and lack of practice, Selkirk managed to utter just one single word: 'Marooned.'

After 52 months of almost uninterrupted solitude on a remote Pacific Island, with nothing but goats and cats for company, Alexander Selkirk's ordeal was finally over. He was warmly welcomed on board the ships, and accounts of his experiences on *Isla Más Atierra* duly recorded. One wonders how his first conversation with William Dampier played out - it certainly had the potential to be an awkward reunion! Selkirk arrived back in England as something of a celebrity, although it didn't take him long to return to his former ways, and in 1713 he was imprisoned for two years for assault. He never returned home to Scotland, and instead he enlisted in the Royal Navy where, somewhat ironically, he was sent to carry out anti-piracy patrols off the west coast of Africa. It was during one of these voyages that he contracted yellow fever and died shortly afterwards, bringing an end to a highly eventful life of 45 years. He was given a simple burial at sea.

Legacy

In 1719, eight years after Selkirk's return to England, the world's most famous novel about a castaway was published. It had taken Daniel Defoe less than six months to write *Robinson Crusoe*, which recounted the fictional narrator's 28-year stay on a remote tropical island in the Caribbean. The similarities between Alexander Selkirk and Robinson Crusoe are difficult to ignore, even if Crusoe's marooning was the result of a shipwreck and included occasional visits from outsiders, before eventually acquiring his own human companion, Friday. Nevertheless, the novel was written at a time when Selkirk-mania was at its peak in Britain, and Defoe neither confirmed nor denied its influence.

Chile also decided that the Selkirk connection was too good

to ignore, and in a bid to improve the tourist appeal of the Juan Fernández islands, they changed the name of *Isla Más Atierra* to **Isla Robinson Crusoe**, and *Isla Más Afuera* to **Isla Alexander Selkirk**. The irony of the latter is that Selkirk never visited that particular island, and with it being located over 100 miles away from *his* island, he was probably unaware of its existence. Selkirk himself unfortunately never wrote an autobiography – if he had kept a diary of all his experiences on *Isla Más Atierra* it would have made for fascinating reading today – meaning that all the accounts of his story were recorded by people who met him in the years following his ordeal.

The retelling of this story wouldn't be complete without mentioning the fate of the *Cinque Ports* and her captain, after he cruelly left Selkirk behind on an uninhabited island in the South Pacific. Convinced that all aboard would be heading to a watery grave if the ship set sail without making significant structural repairs, Selkirk was proved absolutely right; the *Cinque Ports* sank off the South American coast within a month of leaving the Juan Fernández islands, and most of those on board drowned. The survivors, including their captain, Thomas Stradling, were captured by the Spanish and spent the next four years in a squalid Peruvian jail, earning their freedom at about the same time as Alexander Selkirk was meeting his rescuers.

4. Mutiny on the *Bounty*

'Islands are places of intrigue. Washed by the greater mysteries of wind and sea, swept over by tides of human events, they accumulate eerie magnetisms that attract the lawless, the eccentric and – it is said – the supernatural; they shelter oddments of civilisation that evolve into involute societies, and their histories are less likely to reflect orderly patterns of culture than mosaics of bizarre circumstance.'

– Anonymous

The real-life mutiny that occurred on HMS *Bounty* in 1789 contains almost every ingredient of a Boys' Own adventure story, and numerous plays, books, and musicals have retold the events to the delight of global audiences ever since. Its continued popularity owes much to the three major Hollywood films that have recounted the episode in their own particular ways, with the major film stars of their day, Clark Gable, Marlon Brando, and Mel Gibson, each interpreting the complex character of Fletcher Christian. So where better to revisit the facts of this swashbuckling adventure than in the very same waters in which they took place?

During the early 1780s, there were ongoing discussions between the British Government and the plantation owners in their colonies in the Caribbean concerning the introduction of breadfruit as a cheap way of feeding their enslaved workers. Breadfruit is a starchy staple food which was first discovered in Melanesia, before later being introduced into neighbouring Polynesia via human migrations. It was eventually agreed that the Royal Navy would organise a dedicated expedition to the South Pacific in order to transport breadfruit saplings from there to the Caribbean, where they were expected to flourish under similar climatic conditions.

Joseph Banks, the prominent naturalist who had sailed with Captain Cook during his first Pacific voyage on HMS *Endeavour*, had collected and recorded thousands of botanical species in Tahiti, making him the British Government's expert on all matters relating to the Pacific. He was also required to select the vessel for this unusual expedition, and despite the Royal Navy owning more than 600 ships at the time, none of them were considered suitable. Instead, they purchased the collier *Bethia* for £1950, before spending over double that amount on refitting her for the voyage and christening her HMS *Bounty*. She was a small, snub-nosed ship that measured just 90 feet long, and the refit meant that even the captain's cabin was turned into a floating nursery in preparation for transporting breadfruit plants halfway around the world. Banks also had strong opinions regarding who should lead this particular expedition, and he chose the 33-year-old Lieutenant William Bligh, who had previously sailed with Captain Cook on his fateful third Pacific voyage and was considered by the Admiralty to be a young protégé of his former mentor. Bligh had witnessed first-hand Cook's skilful management of both his own crew and the indigenous communities that they encountered, and he also knew the South Pacific relatively well. However, due to the small size of the ship and the nature of the expedition, he was not promoted to the rank of Commander for this voyage, and being overlooked in this way affected him both financially and authoritatively. Lieutenant Bligh would be referred to as 'Captain' by his crew only out of courtesy, but it was to prove an important oversight by the Navy.

Bligh's orders on this occasion were relatively simple: to sail from England to Tahiti, but instead of going via the Cape of Good Hope, he was told to take the quicker route via Cape Horn, despite those waters still being relatively uncharted and the unpredictable nature of the seas around the southern tip of South America. After collecting 700 breadfruit plants from Tahiti, the *Bounty* was to continue sailing westwards in order for Bligh to personally map the Endeavour Strait, a thin stretch of water off the northernmost tip of Australia, and whose treacherous layout was preventing the British from gaining access to the east coast of Australia. Once the survey was complete, the *Bounty* was to transport the breadfruit plants to the West Indies and from there make her way back to England, in a voyage expected to last approximately two years.

Bligh assembled much of his crew from sailors that he already knew, and who, it must be stated, were happy to sail with him again. Others found their way to HMS *Bounty* by personal recommendations or were simply allured by the idea of the South Pacific, and of Tahiti in particular. Bligh selected a distant family friend, Fletcher Christian, to be his Master's mate, bringing the ship's total crew to 46, including two botanists appointed and paid for by Banks. Conditions on board would have been severely cramped given the small size of ship, but nevertheless spirits were high in October 1787 as they sailed down the River Thames bound for the South Pacific.

The outbound voyage to Tahiti was beset with problems from the start; bad weather meant that it took them over three weeks to sail the short distance from London to the English south coast, and they were then kept in Portsmouth waiting for their final sailing orders to arrive from the Admiralty. They watched in despair as ship after ship departed in fine weather, knowing full well that as each week passed, the window for good conditions around Cape Horn was slowly closing. The seas at the southernmost point of South America are most favourable during the austral summer months of January and February, and no experienced sailor would ever consider taking on the Horn much after April. Given that it was a journey of approximately four months from England to South America, Bligh was becoming increasingly concerned by the delays. By late November the *Bounty* had finally received her sailing orders, only for bad weather to postpone their departure by another three weeks. They eventually set sail on 23rd December 1787, already several months behind schedule.

Their passage south was further disrupted by severe storms in the North Atlantic, and Bligh was forced to call in at Tenerife in order to perform urgent repairs to the ship. From Tenerife they made good progress south, and finally sighted the snow-capped mountains of Patagonia in late March 1788. They hoped for a swift and uneventful passage around the southernmost peninsula, but instead were battered by storms that Bligh recorded as having *'exceeded anything I had met with, and a sea higher than I had ever seen before.'* They struggled against the ferocious conditions for almost a month, and despite suffering no loss of life amongst the crew or any significant damage to the ship, they had made no forward progress whatsoever, and Bligh knew that by persevering he was putting the entire expedition at risk. He was left with no choice but to abandon Cape Horn, and instead sail to Tahiti via the Cape of Good Hope and Australia, a detour that would add some 10,000 miles and approximately four months to their journey.

On 27th October 1788, the *Bounty* finally arrived at her anchorage on the northern coast of Tahiti, over ten months after setting sail from England. First-hand reports of the island's beauty and its uninhibited womenfolk would have been well known among the ship's crew, and anticipation on board was at fever pitch as they coasted into Matavai Bay, their home for the next few weeks. After an exuberant welcome by the Tahitians and a lavish exchange of gifts on both sides, Bligh set to work immediately by appointing Fletcher Christian to lead the shore party entrusted with collecting breadfruit from the island's interior. Breadfruit trees existed in large numbers all over the island, and the Tahitians found it very unusual that the British should sail halfway around the world to collect a plant which they considered to be of questionable value. However, there was a problem: neither Banks nor the onboard botanists had known that there was a specific season in the year for breadfruit propagation, and that due to their prolonged voyage from England, they had now missed it. Much to Bligh's horror, their intended one-month stay in this tropical utopia, with all of its carnal temptations, was now going to become almost half a year.

With so much time spent on Tahiti, it was only natural that most of the sailors established romantic relationships with Tahitian women, with some even going as far as getting 'married' to their partners. Many of the crew became deeply embedded in the local culture, with several of them learning to speak the Tahitian language fluently and decorating their bodies with extensive Polynesian tattoos. On 5th April 1789, after more than five months in these idyllic surroundings, Bligh finally gave the order for the *Bounty* to weigh anchor and for the sea passage to the West Indies to begin. Ever the loyal servant to the Admiralty, Bligh had exceeded the 700 plants asked of him by Joseph Banks, and the *Bounty* left Tahiti with over 1,000 healthy breadfruit plants on board, making the ship's quarters even more cramped than had ever been intended. The men's spirits were further tested by having to bid farewell to months of unsupervised freedom and return to the regimented life on board one of His Majesty's Ships. Lieutenant Bligh had also changed during those five months, as he watched his men integrate themselves ever closer with their Tahitian hosts, while he remained a distant and solitary figure on board the *Bounty*. Shortly before setting sail, three of the crew had been caught attempting to desert in one of the ship's longboats and Bligh had no choice but to have them flogged. The general drop in standards of the men's behaviour was becoming a growing concern for the inexperienced captain.

Mutiny

On the evening of 27th April, while the *Bounty* was sailing close to the island of Tofua in modern-day Tonga, an argument broke out on board between William Bligh and Fletcher Christian, with the captain accusing his now second-in-command of having stolen from his personal stockpile of coconuts. Bligh had become increasingly distrustful of the entire crew ever since Tahiti, and he was known to have a violent temper that could erupt at the slightest provocation. On this occasion, Fletcher Christian was equally incensed at having been so publicly humiliated by his captain, and he spent most of that night brooding over their unsavoury altercation. His initial reaction was to take one of the longboats and leave the *Bounty* there and then, but he was calmed down by his fellow crewmembers and subsequently persuaded to consider an even more radical solution to their problem. By early the next morning his mind was made up, and together with a group of armed supporters, they stormed into Bligh's cabin, woke him up, and dragged him up onto the deck. There, they tied him up to one of the masts and announced that they were relieving him of command of the ship. The most serious crime that could be committed on the high seas had just taken place on HMS *Bounty*: Mutiny!

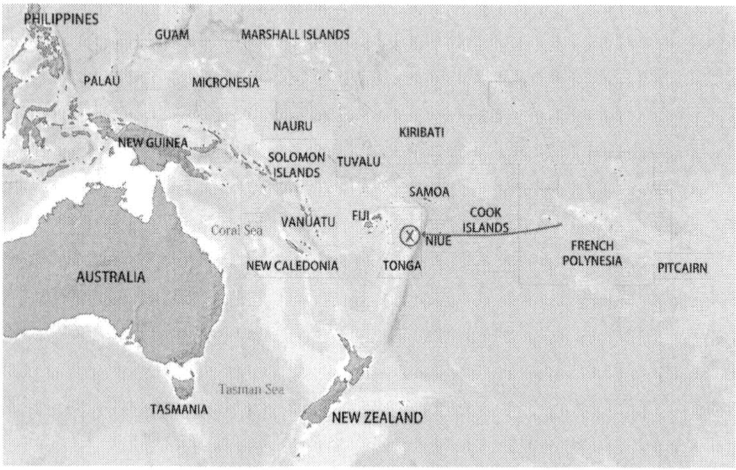

The crew were quickly made to choose between William Bligh and Fletcher Christian, and those who decided to stay with their captain were forced off the *Bounty* and into one of the ship's longboats. Bligh and 18 of those loyal to him were crammed into a rowing boat measuring 23 x 7 feet, which now sat just inches above the waterline. The former captain pleaded desperately to Christian's human side and to their previous friendship, reminding him that '*you have dandled my children on your knee.*' Perhaps moved by Bligh's pleas, Christian agreed to give the group some basic provisions, a sextant, and his own personal compass, without which he would have been condemning those in the longboat to certain death. The mutineers ridiculed Bligh and his loyalists, gleefully throwing every single breadfruit plant that had been so painstakingly collected on Tahiti into the sea, before finally cutting the rope that connected the two vessels. Adrift and alone in the enormity of the Pacific Ocean, and with barely enough food to last for a few days, Lieutenant William Bligh now faced the greatest challenge of his entire career.

In what is still considered to be one of the most remarkable accomplishments in British naval history, Lieutenant Bligh successfully guided their tiny boat over 4,000 miles across the Pacific, navigating all the way from Tofua to Kupang, a Dutch settlement on the island of Timor (in modern-day Indonesia). Despite spending an astonishing 48 days at sea, and only stopping very briefly at a few islands along the way in order to restock with freshwater (Bligh didn't trust the inhabitants of unknown Pacific Islands), he managed to bring the entire group safely to the port of Batavia, from where they were eventually all able to catch ships back to Europe. Upon Bligh's own return to England, news of the mutiny and of their remarkable open-boat voyage had already preceded him, and the Royal Navy was looking for swift retribution against the perpetrators. An Admiralty court-martial soon cleared Bligh of any personal responsibility for the mutiny, and together they drew up a list of all those who had participated in the terrible crime.

Under the command of Captain Edward Edwards, a crew was assembled to hunt down the missing mutineers and bring them to justice, and HMS *Pandora* was chosen for this unique mission. Edwards was provided with a full complement of 134 men, including Thomas Hayward, who had been on the *Bounty* with Bligh, and had loyally accompanied him on their torturous journey to Timor. They also carried with them enough supplies for not only their own voyage, but also for the return voyage of the *Bounty* from Tahiti, since they were fully expecting to escort her back to England with them. In November 1790 the *Pandora* set sail from Portsmouth for South America, following the same route that had proved so problematic for Bligh three years earlier, and by March they had successfully rounded Cape Horn and were making their way into the Pacific. Once they arrived in Tahiti, five of the *Bounty* mutineers immediately gave themselves up to the British authorities, and a further nine were rounded up during the following month. They were all imprisoned inside a makeshift cell on the quarterdeck, soon christened 'Pandora's Box', and Captain Edwards learned from the prisoners that two other mutineers had been killed fighting each other, while HMS *Bounty* containing Fletcher Christian and eight others had not been seen for over 18 months.

In May the *Pandora* left Tahiti with the 14 mutineers in irons, and sailed westwards in order to search for the missing *Bounty* and her crew. Three fruitless months followed, during which time not a single trace of the ship or the mutineers was ever found, before disaster struck and the *Pandora* smashed into the Great Barrier Reef, sinking almost immediately. Thirty-five men drowned, including four of the mutineer prisoners, and the survivors had no choice but to take to the ship's longboats and sail for Timor, where they arrived 16 gruelling days later. For Thomas Hayward this was the second open boat voyage to Timor that he'd been forced to endure in as many years, and he must have been utterly sick of anything to do with HMS *Bounty* by now!

Captain Edwards managed to return to England with just 78 of his original crew of 134 men, as well as 10 of the 14 mutineers who had been apprehended in Tahiti. The mutineers all faced a court-martial upon their arrival, and those whom Bligh confirmed had been loyal to him at the moment of the mutiny but had been forced to remain on the *Bounty*, received full pardons. Several of the guilty mutineers were either acquitted on legal technicalities or granted royal reprieves, but three of them were sentenced to death for their crimes and hanged from the mainsail of the Navy's flagship for every British sailor to see.

It was expected that the court-martials would put an end to the whole saga of HMS *Bounty*, and certainly within the Admiralty it was considered a closed case, despite nine mutineers remaining at large somewhere in the Pacific and still in possession of a ship belonging to the Royal Navy. From 1803 onwards, Britain was heavily involved in the Napoleonic Wars with France and Spain, and interest in the fate of the *Bounty* soon disappeared. No subsequent search for the ship was ever carried out, and it was assumed that the mutineers must have all either died or been shipwrecked, since the *Pandora* had found no sign of them whatsoever.

Discovery

On 6th February 1808, the crew of the American whaling ship *Topaz*, under the command of Captain Mayhew Folger, caught sight of an island in the South Pacific that didn't appear on any of their charts. Folger correctly guessed that it must be the same island that had been sighted by the crew of HMS *Swallow* in 1767 and named after the ship's 15-year-old midshipman, Robert Pitcairn. The island was recorded as being uninhabited, therefore Folger's surprise only grew when he approached the coastline and saw plumes of smoke rising from the interior, confirming a very definite human presence. Shortly afterwards, a group of tanned young men that Folger assumed must be Spanish, paddled out to greet their visitors in an outrigger canoe, laden with gifts of fresh fish and local fruits. The crew of the *Topaz* were stunned when the young men called out in perfect King's English and asked them where they were from, to which Folger replied they were from England, since he doubted that they would have heard of America by then. One of the young men enquired if they had known his father, Fletcher Christian, to which Folger replied that he did not, before the same young man followed up by asking whether they had heard of Captain Bligh, with whom his father had once sailed. And with that single question addressed to the American crew of the whaling ship *Topaz*, one of the world's greatest maritime mysteries had finally been solved, bringing an end to 16 years of uncertainty regarding the outcome of the mutiny on the *Bounty*. The young man addressing them was Thursday October Christian, whose naming had followed the common Polynesian practice of commemorating an important event at the time of his birth, or in this case, its day and month.

The crew of the *Topaz* was welcomed ashore, and Folger eventually met with the island's last surviving mutineer, John Adams, despite his reluctance to be seen by any outsiders for fear that he would be arrested and returned to England in chains. Once Folger had convinced him that he had no such intentions, Adams invited the captain to join him in their small settlement and so began recounting the events that had taken place ever since the fateful day of 28th April 1789.

The mutiny revisited

Once Bligh had departed in the longboat together with 18 of those loyal to him (or perhaps more loyal to the Crown and to seeing England again), Fletcher Christian immediately appointed himself the new commander of the *Bounty*. Initially, the mutineers had intended to sail straight back to Tahiti and to the welcoming arms of their partners, but knowing that this was the first place where a search party would come looking for them, they only visited Tahiti very briefly in order to replenish their supplies. From Tahiti they sailed south for about 350 miles to the coral atoll of Tubuai, where they set to work building a defensive fort, patriotically named Fort George after the British king, to protect themselves from the local Tubuaians, with whom they had a strained relationship from the outset. Local politics on small islands can be convoluted affairs, and the crew of the *Bounty* had unwittingly stumbled upon a complex power struggle that was playing out at the time, and they had inadvertently sided with the weaker of the two chiefs. After three difficult months involving several bloody battles with the locals, Fletcher Christian finally took the decision to take the *Bounty* and her crew to another island, in the hope of finding somewhere more peaceful to settle. They instinctively returned to Tahiti once more, this time to restock their provisions and offload the 16 men amongst Christian's crew who by now had become disillusioned with their new leader; they opted instead for a peaceful life in Tahiti and to wait for the Royal Navy to come and find them, fully aware of the consequences. Those men spent a further 18 months on Tahiti, before the *Pandora* arrived and detained the entire group, with only ten of them ever seeing England again.

The crew of the *Bounty* had now been reduced to just nine mutineers (including Fletcher Christian), as well as three Tahitian males who they employed as servants, and 12 Tahitian females who had all been brought along as partners, one for each man. However, when three additional Tahitian male stowaways were discovered soon after they left Tahiti, Christian decided to let them stay on board, perhaps believing that the additional manpower would be of assistance later. What it actually did was to upset the ratio of males to females in the group, the consequences of which would prove fatal when they eventually settled on their new home.

For two months Christian and his crew scoured the Pacific for a suitable island on which to hide from the British authorities, who would have been alerted to the mutiny by now and well on their way to apprehend them. The mutineers initially searched to the west of Tahiti, amongst the numerous isles of Tonga, Fiji, and the Cook Islands, but failed to find anywhere that met their requirements, namely a secluded island where 27 foreigners could live inconspicuously. At some point during the search, Fletcher Christian was made aware of the uninhabited island of Pitcairn, located 1,400 miles to the east of Tahiti, and he decided that this was an option worth investigating. When the crew of HMS *Swallow* had discovered Pitcairn for the first time, they were unable to land due to rough seas, and so the ship's captain, Philip Carteret, had marked the island on his charts and left. James Cook tried to find Pitcairn at the same coordinates six years later but was unable to locate it; he suspected that it lay further to the east of where he was looking, but an outbreak of scurvy amongst the crew forced him to abandon his search and make his way to Tahiti instead. Fletcher Christian followed the same route as Cook, and likewise failed to find land at the position that Carteret had recorded. Since few of the 18th century explorers were sailing with chronometers that kept accurate time, they consequently had difficulties calculating their exact longitudinal positions, and it wasn't unusual for them to make errors in recording the location of islands. Fletcher Christian suspected this to be the case, and therefore continued sailing along the same latitude until, as he correctly predicted, the island of Pitcairn finally appeared in front of them.

The party of 27 disembarked the *Bounty* for the last time and began exploring the new island. Despite its small size (Pitcairn has an area of just over 2 square miles), they found it to be lush, fertile, and possess an abundance of wild fruit and freshwater. The island had been settled by Polynesians in approximately AD 800 and then abandoned in about 1400, meaning that it had been uninhabited for almost 400 years. Best of all, it was misplaced on the same charts that the British Admiralty would be using to search for them. Soon after their arrival, the mutineers proceeded to burn the *Bounty*, for fear that the obviously British ship would reveal their hiding place. This was a highly controversial decision, and not one apparently shared by all of the mutineers, since the *Bounty* also represented their only means of escape from Pitcairn. They had voluntarily committed to spending the rest of their lives on this tiny island, and any notion that it was going to be a utopian paradise for the new settlers quickly disappeared.

Fletcher Christian struggled to retain his authority over the assorted group once on Pitcairn - ship's rules apparently no longer applied on land - and the first decision he took was to divide up the island into nine equal parts, one for each mutineer and his female partner, but completely ignoring the needs of the male Tahitians. Furthermore, when the wife of one of the mutineers fell to her death collecting seabirds' eggs, he simply replaced her by taking one of the other 'available' Tahitian women. It is not surprising, therefore, that animosity soon began growing between the Tahitians and their British counterparts, and plans for murderous revenge slowly took seed. As the months passed, so this isolated society gradually descended into anarchy, and Fletcher Christian became progressively more reclusive and morose. He would withdraw to a cliffside cave known today as Christian's Cave, where he presumably lamented the decisions that had brought him to this island and to his inescapable predicament. He must have cast his mind back to his family in England, and perhaps even to his former friend William Bligh, and the fact that he would never get to see any of them ever again.

A series of violent murders began taking place on the island, and within several years of the group's arrival, every single one of the Tahitian men had been killed, as well as seven of the nine mutineers, including Fletcher Christian. It is said that he was among the first of the British to be murdered, viciously bludgeoned over the head by an aggrieved Tahitian while he tended to his taro plantation. Just two of the mutineers remained, and Ned Young used the Bible from the *Bounty* to teach John Adams how to read and write, and also converted him to Christianity. When Young later died from asthma, Adams was left as the island's sole patriarch, dutifully caring for multiple women and raising numerous offspring in the English language and grounded in the Christian faith. And this is how he came to be recounting this incredible series of events to Mayhew Folger in 1808, and an adventure that even the well-travelled American must have struggled to comprehend.

When news eventually reached the British Admiralty about the one surviving *Bounty* mutineer, he was pardoned in absentia due to the reports of his reformed behaviour on the island, and the fact that there was little interest in revisiting the mutiny after so many years. John Adams died on 5th March 1829 at the age of 65 and is the only one of the mutineers whose burial place on Pitcairn has so far been identified.

Pitcairn Today

Pitcairn remains as isolated and inaccessible as ever and can only be reached by the occasional cruise or infrequent cargo ship from the island of Mangareva in French Polynesia. Given the island's unique history, it remains a British Overseas Territory and the last UK protectorate in all of the Pacific. The capital of Pitcairn, Adamstown, was named after John Adams, and many of the 50 or so people who still live on the island today are direct descendants of the mutineers and their Tahitian partners. Despite the island's lush and tropical appearance, it remains an extremely challenging place to live, and with an ageing population and considerable difficulties in attracting new people to settle there, the island's future looks to be increasingly uncertain.

As for William Bligh, his name was forever connected with the unfortunate events of the *Bounty*, and his naval career never fully recovered. His reputation was permanently tarnished by the belief that he'd been unnecessarily strict and even cruel towards his crew, when in reality there were numerous factors that led to the mutiny, far beyond any shortcomings in Bligh's leadership style. As the only officer on board HMS *Bounty*, he had been given almost no support by his superiors, with the Admiralty having failed to provide him with any marines, who essentially served as the captain's security detail during long voyages. It is worth noting that on each of the three Pacific voyages undertaken by James Cook, he never sailed with fewer than 12 marines.

Four years after the mutiny, Bligh successfully led a second mission to transplant breadfruit from Tahiti to the West Indies on board HMS *Providence*, and despite its initial unpopularity, breadfruit has now become an integral part of Caribbean cuisine. In 1805, (now) Captain William Bligh retired from the Royal Navy and was appointed Governor of New South Wales in Australia, yet again on the personal recommendation of Sir Joseph Banks. Bligh walked into a highly complex political situation in what was effectively still a penal colony, and in 1808 – coincidentally, the same year that John Adams was revealing his secrets to Mayhew Folger on Pitcairn – Bligh was ousted from office and physically dragged out of Government House. He was subsequently forced to spend two years on a British warship anchored in Sydney Harbour, awaiting further support to arrive from England. Often referred to as Bligh's second mutiny, it brought the curtain down on a long and difficult career, best summed up by the epitaph on his gravestone: *In Caelo Quies* – 'In Heaven there is Peace.'

Today's permanent population on one of the most remote islands in the world is an enduring legacy of the mutiny which took place on HMS *Bounty*, and despite the wide-ranging issues currently facing the people of Pitcairn, it would be a significant loss if the island were ever to return to its uninhabited status. Pitkern, the language spoken by the island's inhabitants, is a unique mix of Tahitian and 18th century English, and perfectly embodies this highly improbable blend of cultures produced by one extraordinary event in the South Pacific.

5. Thor Heyerdahl & *Kon-Tiki*

'The Kon-Tiki expedition opened my eyes to what the ocean really is: it is a conveyor and not an isolator. The ocean has been man's highway from the days he built the first buoyant ships, long before he tamed the horse, invented wheels, and cut roads through the virgin jungles.'

– Thor Heyerdahl

For readers of a certain age today, the books of Thor Heyerdahl formed a memorable part of their childhood, and there is no doubting the influence that his stories have had on an entire generation. The adventures that he undertook must have appeared as unbridled escapism to those living in the austere years following the end of WW2, at the same time as inspiring his readers to explore the most far-flung corners of the world as soon as they were adults. When speaking with numerous visitors on Easter Island, I was amazed to discover how many of them had been inspired to visit after reading the books of Thor Heyerdahl as children, and had waited a near lifetime to do so. Conversely, the scientific community has been a consistent critic of the methodology employed by Heyerdahl and the conclusions that he reached, and this has been even more notable due to his global notoriety and fame. Whatever one's opinion of him, there is no denying the impact that Heyerdahl had on all of the countries he visited, particularly the islands in the South Pacific, and he remains one of the most famous Norwegians to this day.

Thor Heyerdahl was born in 1914 in the whaling town of Larvik, some 80 miles south of Oslo. His father owned a small brewery, while his mother managed the local museum, a fact that seemingly played an important part in the direction that her young son's life would later take. From an early age, Thor displayed a keen curiosity for the natural world and even set up a small zoological museum in their family home, before later pursuing his undergraduate studies in Zoology & Geography at the University of Oslo. Within his studies, Heyerdahl took a particular interest in the history and cultures of Polynesia, and he was soon planning to spend a year on a remote South Sea Island in order to learn how certain species of plants and animals had arrived there. In reality, he was desperate to break free from the shackles of 1930s Europe, and while at university he had also met his future wife, Liv, who was equally fascinated by the idea of escaping from the modern world and going back to nature.

Fatu Hiva

Thor and Liv married on Christmas Eve 1936, and the very next day travelled to Marseille in order to catch the steamship to French Polynesia. This first expedition was sponsored by both of their parents, but much more than being a honeymoon of any kind, it was intended to be a year-long academic field trip before they returned to Norway and settled down into more 'normal' lives. Heyerdahl later admitted that they hadn't in fact ever intended to return, and that if they managed to survive by themselves on their desert island, then they planned to stay there for the rest of their lives. Aged just 22 and 20 respectively, Thor and Liv were an idealistic young couple who shared a disillusionment with modern society and felt that mankind's supposed progress in the world was in fact taking it backwards. They both wished to demonstrate that a simple life was a more favourable alternative, and thus inspire a generation of young people to 'return to nature' too.

They selected the island of Fatu Hiva in the Marquesas group of French Polynesia for their experiment, and despite neither of them ever having been there before, they knew that it was both remote and lacking in significant infrastructure. It had a local population of just 500 people, but the island was large enough that they would be able to live away from the small community, and it possessed adequate fertile soil and drinking water for them to live self-sufficiently. In order to get there, Thor and Liv sailed for six weeks from France to Tahiti, where they had to wait for the next cargo ship that would be calling in at the Marquesas. During those weeks spent waiting on the main island of French Polynesia, the locals who learned of their plan insisted on teaching them the basic skills for surviving on a tropical island, such as how to catch crayfish, climb palm trees, and cook using the traditional Polynesian method. Three weeks later they had managed to secure a space on the deck of a goods ship bound for Fatu Hiva. The captain was an Englishman who had spent many years sailing around the islands of Polynesia and by now had become jaded by the region and its people; he tried several times to persuade the young couple to abandon their crazy idea and return to Tahiti with him, but they hadn't come all this way to give up now. After passing Fatu Hiva's majestic Hanavave Bay, he reluctantly set them down at the main settlement of Omoa and promised to come back for them in a year's time.

The reality of the Heyerdahls' South Seas fantasy proved to be much more of an ordeal than either of them had ever envisaged, and despite the idyllic location of their bamboo cabin, they felt continually threatened by their surroundings, whether it was the intrusive wild boar or the unrelenting insects. They had chosen to stay on the uninhabited side of the island and as far away as possible from the small resident population, partly in order to isolate themselves from society, but also because of a severe outbreak of elephantiasis amongst the locals which was known to be highly transmissible. Despite the abundance of fresh fruit such as mango, coconut, and breadfruit, the couple still depended on the locals for meat and other 'luxury' items that they were unable to obtain for themselves. While these interactions began well, and the locals found the new arrivals to be an entertaining novelty, as the months wore on the relationship began to sour, and the young couple spent their final few weeks on Fatu Hiva hiding in a cave, out of sight of the islanders.

One morning Liv woke up and discovered that she had been badly bitten by a centipede during the night, and they both decided that they had been there long enough and that it was time to go home. They spent the following days scanning the horizon, and when they sighted the unmistakeable white sails of an inter-island schooner headed for Omoa, they gathered up their few remaining belongings and hurried towards the island's main settlement. They managed to secure a passage to Tahiti, and from there they caught the steamer back to France, before finally returning home to Norway. An important factor not mentioned by Heyerdahl in his book is that Liv must have realised that she was pregnant in those final months of their stay on Fatu Hiva, and this would have greatly influenced their decision to go home. Thor Jr. was born in September 1938, by which time they were safely back in Norway and seemingly embarking on a more settled lifestyle, or so their parents presumably hoped!

The Heyerdahls spent a total of 15 months in the Marquesas, during which time they succeeded in proving that it was still possible for two westerners to live an Adam & Eve existence, before they ultimately became disenchanted by the allure of 'paradise' and began missing their families and friends. While Heyerdahl did very little of his own scientific research on Fatu Hiva, his curiosity was aroused by the presence of the sweet potato on the island, a starchy vegetable that is usually only found in South America. Furthermore, he was surprised to observe the wind blowing from the east for the entire duration of their stay, and noticed that the east side of the island was constantly battered by waves, while the west side was always calm. Ironically, these were the two most significant discoveries made by Heyerdahl during that entire period, and together they would form the basis of many of his subsequent experiments and theories.

Shortly after their return, the couple wrote a brief account of their adventure in Norwegian, but it wasn't until 1974 that Heyerdahl published the book *Fatu Hiva: Back to Nature* in English, and it remains a wonderful account of their time in remotest Polynesia, an experience that would be almost impossible to replicate today. Heyerdahl spent most of WW2 with the Norwegian resistance in its struggle against the occupying Nazis, however these enforced years in Norway and the economic slump that followed, did little to curb his wanderlust and his enthusiasm for yet another adventure, and one that would ultimately launch him to worldwide fame.

The *Kon-Tiki*

In 1947, Heyerdahl assembled a crew of six Scandinavians, including himself, to try to prove his theory that indigenous South Americans could have discovered and settled parts of Polynesia during the pre-Columbian era. This would convincingly explain how the sweet potatoes that he'd seen in Fatu Hiva had reached the island, in stark contrast to the generally accepted theory that the human colonisation of the Pacific had originated in Southeast Asia. Organising this type of expedition just two years after the largest war in Europe had finished was an audacious task, and Heyerdahl required a team in which each crewmember offered a unique skillset, as well as the resilience to survive such a long and dangerous voyage. He felt it was important that the individuals didn't know each other particularly well beforehand, as too much familiarity could lead to carelessness, and there would be numerous weeks at sea for them to get to know each other better. Heyerdahl's telegram inviting his friend Torstein Raaby to join the expedition is a wonderful example of 1940s forthrightness and understatement:

> AM GOING TO CROSS PACIFIC ON A WOODEN RAFT TO SUPPORT A THEORY THAT THE SOUTH SEA ISLANDS WERE PEOPLED FROM PERU. WILL YOU COME? I GUARANTEE NOTHING BUT A FREE TRIP TO PERU AND THE SOUTH SEA ISLANDS AND BACK, BUT YOU WILL FIND GOOD USE FOR YOUR TECHNICAL ABILITIES ON THE VOYAGE. REPLY AT ONCE.

Likewise, the answer that he received the following day was everything that Heyerdahl could have hoped for when planning a near-suicidal transoceanic voyage on a balsawood raft:

`COMING. TORSTEIN.`

The six crewmembers met up together in Peru, from where they hoped to source the materials for their traditional raft, the design of which was based on illustrations recorded by the Spanish *Conquistadores*, who had witnessed the native South Americans and their embarkations first-hand. The validity of the experiment depended entirely on their using the same construction materials that had been available in pre-Columbian times, in this case large trunks of native balsawood and heavy ropes made from hemp. They were unable to use older, drier logs due to the amount of water that they would absorb over the course of the voyage thus causing the raft to sink, so the crew travelled to the rainforest in Ecuador instead, where they found younger, green trees and transported them to Lima by sea.

Their primitive raft consisted of nine large balsawood logs stripped of their bark, into which they carved deep grooves and inserted heavy ropes, thus lashing everything tightly together. Nine traversal logs were placed on top of the balsawood, and finally the whole surface was covered with a bamboo flooring. Not a single nail, screw, or rivet was used to hold the raft together, as dictated by boatbuilding techniques prior to European contact. During the construction process, they were met with a regular stream of naysayers who felt that they would be lucky to make it even halfway to Polynesia before their raft broke up under the force of the ocean, and the Peruvian Navy even made Heyerdahl sign a waiver that absolved them of any responsibility in the event of their disappearance. While they put the finishing touches to their vessel, they also received plenty of curious visitors, and there was no doubt that the voyage was appealing to the imagination of a wide audience. It was the first expedition to have been organised purely for adventure's sake since the end of the Second World War, and there was also considerable interest amongst the local Peruvians, who were intrigued by the idea that their ancestors may have even reached Polynesia too.

The raft that would hopefully transport the Scandinavians across the Pacific was christened after a god from Incan culture, Kon-Tiki, whose name shared an uncanny resemblance to that of the Marquesan deities, *tiki*, which Heyerdahl had heard during his stay in Fatu Hiva. He was unable to accept that this wasn't further proof of direct human contact between the two regions, despite the extremely limited cultural and linguistic links in every other aspect and the vast distance that separated them.

With final preparations completed, the *Kon-Tiki* slipped out of her berth at the port of Callao on the night of 28th April 1947. A tugboat was required to pull the raft 50 miles out to sea in order to carry her clear of the commercial shipping lanes that ran parallel to the country's coast, but from a scientific perspective this single action greatly affected the integrity of the experiment. By having the raft mechanically towed through the Humboldt current, they drastically altered the conditions from those faced by the indigenous Indians, and as a consequence the *Kon-Tiki* probably took a more southerly track across the Pacific.

As soon as they had been released into the open ocean, the crew had to quickly adapt to the behaviour of the raft and perfect their basic survival skills. They brought 1,000 litres of drinking water with them and a mix of local fruit and vegetables from Peru; however, they would rely on catching fish for most of their food, something that proved to be much easier than even they could have imagined. Schools of flying fish would dart in and out of the water around their raft, and each night many unfortunate ones would land on the deck of the *Kon-Tiki* instead of their intended watery splashdown. The chef's job each morning was simply to walk around the bamboo floor and collect the stranded fish, one of which even found its way into a crewmember's sleeping bag! The men's diet was supplemented by larger fish such as tuna, mahi-mahi, and swordfish, and even the occasional shark in order to prevent these aggressive animals from attacking them. Prior to the start of the expedition, Heyerdahl had also met with various senior American dignitaries, who requested that he use the long voyage to test the U.S. Army's field rations for them, resulting in two of the crew apparently having to live on nothing but powdered food and dry biscuits for the entire journey. One suspects, however, that the abundance of fresh fish each day might have proven too great a temptation to resist!

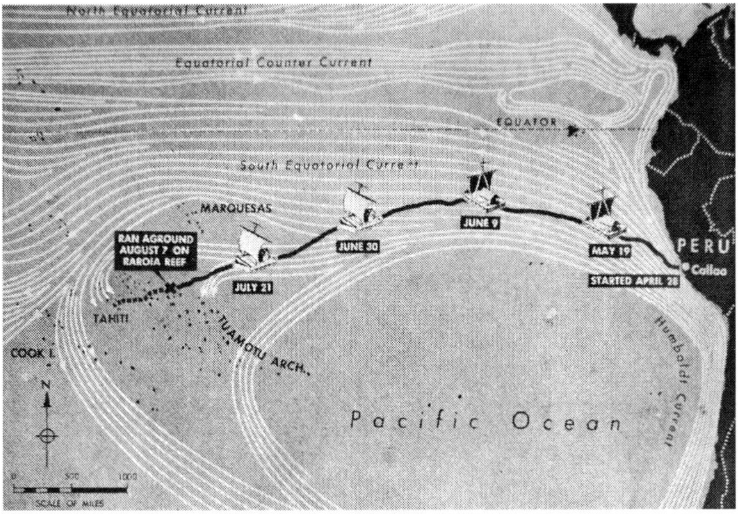

Once underway, the prevailing winds and currents were pushing them westwards at a good speed, and they managed to travel over 80 miles in one 24-hour period alone. They calculated their speed by dropping a small piece of wood from the bow of the raft and measuring the time it took to reach the stern. Communication with the outside world was equally unsophisticated, but with two of the men having worked as radio operators during WW2, they were able to use the onboard wireless to transmit occasional updates. These messages were picked up by various amateur radio enthusiasts across the Pacific and further afield, and relayed to the Norwegian Embassy in Washington, which was overseeing the expedition's progress.

The unexpected speed of the raft almost proved fatal for two of the crewmembers who had rowed a short distance away in order to do some filming, only to find themselves suddenly unable to make it back to the raft. Since much of the funding for the expedition depended on the production of a documentary at the end of it, they had brought a small dinghy along with them which they would occasionally use in order to get some action footage of their progress. However, on this occasion the two men were alarmed to discover that they were quickly being left behind by the *Kon-Tiki* and were unable to row fast enough to catch up with their rapidly-disappearing companions. Minutes of frantic paddling followed, but with no sea anchor or any other way of slowing the *Kon-Tiki* down, there was very little that the crew could do to help them. The exhausted pair were eventually able to get themselves back to within a rope's length of the raft and could be pulled back in, but no one was ever allowed to row away from the *Kon-Tiki* again without being securely attached by ropes.

Fierce storms and rough seas were perhaps the greatest threat to the crew's survival, often causing the *Kon-Tiki* to be tossed about violently on the ocean. On one occasion, an enormous wave washed one of the crewmembers overboard, and despite his frantic efforts to keep up, he was unable to swim fast enough to stay alongside the raft. He desperately tried to grab the steering oar that protruded from the back of the stern but to no avail, and within seconds he was vanishing from sight, to the utter horror of those who remained on board. While they desperately tried to untie the dinghy before their friend disappeared forever, one of the men realised that the whole process was taking far too long and bravely dived in after him, holding nothing but a rope in his hand. Despite each man continually losing sight of the other in between the enormous waves, they somehow managed to link up and were both eventually dragged back on board; it had been an extremely close brush with death and a very real reminder of the constant dangers that surrounded them in the middle of the ocean.

By the 45th day the *Kon-Tiki* had covered over half of its intended route, and the crew's dreams of reaching Polynesia were finally starting to look like a possibility. Shortly before leaving Peru, they had been given a green macaw parrot to take on their journey by a generous well-wisher, and despite their initial reluctance for any additional passengers, Lorita proved to be an excellent sailing companion. Like several of the men, she suffered from acute seasickness at the start of the voyage, but once they found their sea legs, she provided great entertainment with her attempts to imitate the Norwegian radio transmissions. She stayed on board for over two months, until one day she was swept overboard by a large wave and never seen again, much to the sorrow of the crew.

Throughout the entire journey they were utterly alone in the vast expanse of the Pacific Ocean, and they never saw a single other ship or person during the whole voyage. Numerous sea creatures accompanied them for various parts of their journey, and while these animals were generally only curious about the unusual object sharing this lonely piece of ocean with them, the crew had to maintain a vigilant lookout all the same. The most threatened they ever felt was when they caught sight of a whale shark, the world's largest fish, swimming beneath their raft; fully aware that with one swish of its tail this docile giant was capable of flipping them completely over, one of the men reluctantly fired a harpoon into the animal's back and managed to scare it away.

The greatest concern during the expedition came from the state of their raft below the waterline and the extent to which the logs were absorbing water and the ropes becoming frayed by the powerful waves. They constructed a long wicker basket which could hold one crewmember at a time, and by using a pair of swimming goggles he was able to frequently inspect the underside of the raft. Since sharks were regular visitors throughout the voyage, the basket offered the diver some basic protection and meant that if he suddenly felt threatened, he could hide inside it while his friends quickly pulled him out of the water. The logs were always noted to be in excellent condition and the ropes undamaged, a testament to the workmanship of the raft's construction and the meticulous preparation by the crew.

With the use of a sextant, the crew were able to take daily positional readings and thus chart their progress across the Pacific, while also estimating when they could expect to catch sight of land for the first time. By late July, small numbers of seabirds began appearing around the raft - an encouraging sign that they might finally be nearing landfall – and finally on August 5th, 99 days after their departure from Peru, Bengt Danielsson bounded down the rope ladder from his perch on the masthead: 'Land ahoy!'. The island in front of them was unmistakably a coral atoll, but they only knew that they were somewhere in the Tuamotu archipelago in French Polynesia. A group of local islanders paddled their canoes out to the raft, providing the crew with their first human contact in over three months, however they were unable to slow the *Kon-Tiki* down or alter its course, and ended up drifting helplessly past the island. The same series of events took place the following day, and it was only when a third island appeared in front of them on the third day that they realised they were heading directly for its fringing coral reef. Rapidly advancing towards this impenetrable natural barrier and with no means of slowing the raft down in order to reduce the impact, they tied down everything on board as best they could in preparation for their first contact with dry land in over 100 days.

Radio transmissions had been difficult throughout the voyage, but just before landfall they managed to make contact with an amateur radio operator in New Zealand. They explained to him that they were about to crash into the reef of an unknown island, and if they didn't make any further transmissions within the next 36 hours, the poor operator was to alert the Norwegian authorities in Washington that the entire crew of the *Kon-Tiki* had perished. After 4,300 miles and 101 days at sea, the six crewmembers braced themselves for impact as their raft was hurled onto the razor-sharp reef by the powerful waves.

Despite the *Kon-Tiki* being almost completely wrecked, all six men survived uninjured, and they quickly gathered up whatever they could salvage and set foot on land for the first time in over three months. They had in fact crashed into an uninhabited corner of the atoll of Raroia, and news of the arrival of six sunburnt Europeans quickly spread amongst the islanders, who came to see these unusual visitors for themselves. Just before the 36 hours were up, the crew successfully sent a radio message that they had indeed survived their meeting with solid ground, and the rest of the world gradually began to hear about the astonishing feat that these six men had achieved. After several weeks spent recovering on Raroia, they patched up the *Kon-Tiki* sufficiently for it to be towed back to Tahiti with them, and they were welcomed on French Polynesia's main island and subsequently back in Norway as global celebrities.

Legacy

Written in 1948, Heyerdahl's account of the voyage still makes for compelling reading today, and the fact that it has sold over 50 million copies and been translated into more than 70 languages is testament to the popularity of this extraordinary story. Despite some of the footage having been destroyed by seawater during their final crash landing, the documentary of the expedition was released in 1950 and won the Oscar for Best Documentary the following year. The story was retold once more in 2012 in a highly dramatised Hollywood version, and despite numerous historical inaccuracies, it was nominated for Best Foreign Language film at both the Oscars and the Golden Globes. Interestingly, each scene in the film was shot twice: once in Norwegian for the domestic market, and then again in English for an international audience.

Despite the obvious success of the expedition, it did very little to alter scientific opinion regarding the settlement of the Pacific, and was given minimal attention by the academic community. While the *Kon-Tiki* demonstrated that drifting from South America to Polynesia was theoretically possible, all of the evidence still pointed to the region's settlement having originated in Southeast Asia. Recent archaeological, linguistic, and particularly human genetic data have all supported this theory, as does the Polynesians' own oral history and the trail of plants and animals that they left behind as they travelled eastwards. The question of how South American plants such as the sweet potato came to be found in Polynesia, the key argument on which Heyerdahl's theory hinged, was answered when they were shown to have been introduced to the region by the Polynesians, after one of their occasional contacts with the native South Americans.

One of the fundamental criticisms of the *Kon-Tiki* expedition was the crew's inability to steer the raft, or to have any real control over the direction in which the forces of nature took it. This had potentially major consequences on the open ocean, where directional errors of just one degree could be the difference between locating an island or not, and also made the steering of the raft particularly problematic when approaching land. Computer models have demonstrated that while some archipelagos consisting of multiple islands could have been settled using drift voyaging, it was almost impossible in the case of outlying islands such as Hawai'i, Easter Island, or New Zealand. It is ironic that many more people today have heard of the *Kon-Tiki* expedition of 1947 than of the *Hokule'a* voyage of 1976, despite the latter successfully completing the first voyage for centuries between major Polynesian island groups using only traditional techniques.

Heyerdahl possessed an incurable wanderlust and an adventurer's spirit that was to last for his entire lifetime. In 1955 he organised the first large-scale archaeological expedition to Easter Island, after his interest had been piqued while passing to the north of the island on board the *Kon-Tiki*. Despite most of his theories from that adventure later being refuted by more scientific techniques, his book about the expedition, *Aku Aku*, is a wonderful account and was instrumental in putting the remote Polynesian island on the world map. During his seven-month stay there, Heyerdahl undertook pioneering excavations of the statues and carried out experiments regarding their transportation, as well as re-erecting the first statue back onto its ceremonial platform after they had all been thrown over during the 18th and 19th centuries. Sadly, Heyerdahl was also easily fooled by the inhabitants of Easter Island, something that he only alludes to briefly in *Aku Aku*; realising that he would pay good money for any artefacts that could be removed from the island, the locals began carving small statues at a frenzied rate and would approach him with offers to take him to secret caves where their ancestors had hidden ancient relics. Heyerdahl initially bought as many of these trinkets as he could, until he finally realised that some of them were in fact far too new to be 'ancient' carvings, and that the locals had been tricking him all along. The statues that he did collect, together with the original *Kon-Tiki* raft, are now on display at the Kon-Tiki Museum in Oslo, which is well worth visiting for anyone interested in Heyerdahl's life and his various adventures.

In 1969, Heyerdahl attempted to sail across the Atlantic Ocean in a reed boat, with the aim of proving that the Ancient Egyptians could have crossed the same body of water and arrived at the New World long before Christopher Columbus. The first voyage, on *Ra I*, reached within 100 miles of the Caribbean coast before the reeds became so waterlogged that they eventually broke apart, requiring the crew to be rescued by a passing yacht. The next year they repeated the expedition, this time using improved materials and techniques for the new raft, and successfully completed the journey between Morocco and Barbados in 57 days on the *Ra II*.

One little-known legacy of the *Kon-Tiki* expedition is the later life of the only Swedish member of the crew, Bengt Danielsson. He had been the chef during the voyage, and as the only person in the team who spoke Spanish, he was also the translator. Whereas all of the other crewmembers returned to live in Europe after the voyage, Danielsson stayed in Polynesia, initially settling on the island of Raroia where the *Kon-Tiki* had crash-landed. Both he and his wife subsequently became prominent campaigners against the nuclear tests being carried out in French Polynesia at the time and were strong critics of French colonialism, ultimately becoming leading experts on almost all subjects related to the Pacific Ocean.

Heyerdahl himself never stopped researching, excavating, and questioning other people's theories, and he was still actively working on solving archaeological riddles well into his eighties. The general criticism levied against him was always that he formed a theory and then looked for evidence to support it, whereas serious scientific study generally works the other way around, beginning with a thorough analysis of all of the available data. He maintained the strong belief that all ancient civilisations were closely connected by the oceans as opposed to being limited by them, and right up until his death in 2002 he remained a prominent figure in highlighting the threats of sea pollution and climate change, the seeds of which may well have been sown during the *Kon-Tiki* expedition.

6. The Mystery of Easter Island

'In the middle of the Great Ocean, in a region where no one ever passes, there is a mysterious and isolated island; there is no land in the vicinity and, for more than eight hundred leagues in all directions, empty and moving vastness surrounds it. It is planted with tall, monstrous statues, the work of some now vanished race, and its past remains an enigma.'

– Pierre Loti

Ever since European explorers first caught sight of this lonely outpost in 1722, no other island in the world has generated quite the same aura of mystery as solitary Easter Island. Possibly the most isolated inhabited island anywhere on the globe, the discovery of hundreds of colossal stone statues all along its coastline led early visitors to marvel at the creativity of its inhabitants, and has since made Rapa Nui (Easter Island's Polynesian name) by far the most studied island in the Pacific. But what do the iconic statues really mean? How were they all carved and subsequently transported across the island? And why was every single one ultimately knocked down and destroyed by the native inhabitants? Despite our ever-improving knowledge of human history, Easter Island remains a fascinating outlier, and many of its mysteries continue to baffle the scientific community even to this day.

The ability of Polynesian scouts to have discovered Easter Island in the first place remains a highly impressive achievement, although even more extraordinary was their ability to have successfully settled the island with a sustainable human population that continues to thrive today. Nevertheless, the island is consistently cited as an example of the mismanagement of natural resources, in which its inhabitants cut down every single tree and the society descended into violent chaos, ultimately leading to their own extinction. However, a more serious examination of the data roundly contradicts this popular version of events and instead reveals that Easter Island was in fact one of the shining success stories of the South Pacific.

Rapa Nui was placed on the world map on 5th April 1722, when three Dutch ships sailing under the command of Jacob Roggeveen sighted an island that didn't appear on any of their charts, and given that the day was Easter Sunday, they named the island 'Paaseiland' (Easter Island in Dutch). They never expected to find people living on such a remote spot and were extremely surprised when several islanders calmly swam out to their anchored ships, displaying no fear whatsoever towards their new visitors. The crew's amazement doubled when they began sailing around the island and saw an almost continuous line of statues erected along the coastline, having never seen carvings of this size or on this scale anywhere before. Ultimately, the initial contact between the native Rapanui and the first known visitors to the island was a disastrous one, in which the Dutch felt increasingly threatened by the behaviour of the locals and the persistent theft of their belongings. They eventually drew their muskets and fired shots into the swelling crowd, killing 12 islanders outright and causing unimaginable confusion amongst their compatriots. Roggeveen sailed hastily away, conscious that he had just stumbled upon one of the world's most unusual cultures, but completely unaware that he had also discovered the eastern edge of the Polynesian triangle.

Easter Island lies at the furthest extreme of a human settlement that spread to nearly every corner of the Pacific, and became the easternmost island to be permanently inhabited by the Polynesians (they only visited South America very occasionally). It is a small, volcanic island with an area of barely 63 square miles and a highest point just 1,700 feet above sea level. However, the Polynesians who first discovered it found something of a South Seas paradise there: palm trees covered more than 70% of the island, thousands of seabirds nested there each year, and most importantly of all, it had three volcanic crater lakes that each contained an abundance of freshwater. There were, however, no land-based animals on Easter Island at that time, and ever since the island had erupted from the sea floor several million years earlier, no fauna had yet found its way there except for the multitude of seabirds. Recognising that the island offered excellent opportunities for fishing and agriculture, the scouts must have returned to their homeland convinced that this was an island very much suitable for settlement.

Months later, a diverse group of Polynesians disembarked from their double-hulled canoes onto the white sand beach of Anakena and so became the first permanent inhabitants of Easter Island. It is generally accepted that this voyage began from either the Marquesas Islands or Mangareva, both in modern-day French Polynesia, although the Rapanui oral history offers very few clues as to why they chose such a remote island on which to settle. The new settlers introduced chickens and rats to their island, but neither dogs nor pigs it seems, suggesting they were constrained either by the limited space on board their canoes, or that these two species didn't survive the month-long sea voyage. The new inhabitants also introduced bananas, taro, and sweet potatoes to the island, as well as the paper mulberry tree, the bark of which was used to make clothing. Recent archaeological studies point to this having been the first and only Polynesian settlement of Easter Island, suggesting that they metaphorically closed the door behind them once they arrived, resulting in over 700 years of total isolation.

Much of today's fascination with Easter Island understandably focuses on the 1,000 or so **moai** (pronounced *'mow-eye'*), the iconic stone statues found only here. Each one was carved in order to represent an important human ancestor, a cultural practice that took place in many other parts of Polynesia (and further afield), but nowhere else did it result in so many statues of such monumental proportions. The moai were carved from soft volcanic rock using stone tools, and could measure anywhere from 3 to 70 feet tall and weigh up to 200 tonnes. Despite its diminutive size, Easter

Island possesses one of the best stone quarries anywhere in the Pacific, as well as an ample supply of basalt and obsidian, both ideal raw materials from which to make stone carving tools. The abundance of these natural resources, together with the instilled cultural beliefs that were introduced by the first settlers on the island, combined to create the perfect conditions for this religious artform to develop, resulting in the megalithic creations for which Easter Island is recognised globally today.

It is clear that the inhabitants of Rapa Nui proudly honoured their dead, more than on almost any other island, and that they went to extreme lengths to preserve their ancestors' *mana* for themselves and for future generations. *Mana* can sometimes be a difficult concept for non-Polynesians to understand, and is not an easy term to translate directly into English, but simply put, it is the spiritual energy and life force contained within a person or an inanimate object which can be freely transferred to others, even after a person's death. Some people acquired their *mana* at birth, such as those born into the royal lineages, while others earned it through the results of their actions, such as successful carvers and fishermen. Much more than just a religious belief system, *mana* was the main philosophy and frame of reference for nearly all Polynesians up until recent times. Understandably, one of the greatest concerns in 21st century Polynesia has been the rapid disappearance of this particular credence, and its replacement by foreign attitudes and values. The way in which modern Polynesian societies balance these two opposing forces will be one of the most interesting challenges facing the people in this region.

Carving

As soon as a person who was considered to possess a large amount of *mana* died on Easter Island, a team of carvers from his or her community went to the stone quarry at Rano Raraku and began etching a representation of that particular ancestor out of the rock. Work on a single statue could take anywhere up to two years to complete, and the finished moai would then have to be transported out of the quarry and across the island, down a series of specially built paved roads. These journeys could sometimes involve hauling the moai distances of up to 20 miles, no mean feat given the size and weight of each statue, before delivering it to the part of the island where the ancestor's tribe was located. Once the statue had arrived, the ancestor's offspring erected it onto a prominent ceremonial platform, or **ahu**, which was generally positioned next to the coastline, in such a way that the moai faced inland and watched over its descendants. There is a common misconception that the moai gazed out to sea, which has seemingly arisen from photographs of the unfinished statues still in the quarry, in contrast to the completed statues erected on their permanent plinths. The moai were sometimes designated to be a single statue on each platform, and at other times groups of moai stood together and shared the same platform. Very little is understood today about why this was the case.

Another widely held belief is that the statues were only carved from the shoulders upwards, and you will often hear people incorrectly referring to the 'heads' of Easter Island. Again, since the most common photographs of the moai are those of the unfinished statues in the quarry, people fail to appreciate that much of the loose sediment produced by the carving process gradually slid down the outer slopes of the quarry and buried many of the statues up to their necks, or in some cases completely. Archaeological excavations in the early 20th century unequivocally confirmed that all of the 'heads' in the quarry were in fact complete statues, buried from their shoulders down to their waists, and since the focus of the island authorities today is quite rightly on the preservation of their cultural patrimony, the covered moai are now all left untouched.

It was believed that a person's *mana* was found in their head and torso, and for this reason it appears that all the statues finished at their waists, as opposed to having legs or any other features. There was also the practical issue that it was much easier to transport and erect an enormous block of stone that presented a flat base, and for these two reasons this stylised and highly distinctive design for representing ancestors was developed. In terms of the gender of the moai, strictly speaking the statues were sexless, but given their square jawlines and unmistakable paunches, we can assume that they were representations of male ancestors. However, about a dozen moai with obvious female features have also been unearthed, confirming that both sexes were in fact honoured.

Transportation & Assembly

The question of how the islanders managed to move these colossal statues long distances across rocky, uneven ground is one that continues to puzzle archaeologists even now. This scientific uncertainty has led to a myriad of possible theories, ranging from the rational to the ridiculous, and not helped by the fact that when the locals were asked by Heyerdahl and others how the moai were transported to their platforms, they replied that the statues simply walked using *mana*. Countless students have speculated about the feasibility of various methods of transportation, from the use of ocean barges to large wooden bipods, and even the participation of UFOs and extra-terrestrials! However, the two most serious explanations can best be summarised as the 'rocking' and the 'rolling' methods:

Rocking involved standing the moai upright while teams of men took it in turns to pull on ropes attached to its head, thus inching the statue forward on its edges in the same way as you might 'walk' a heavy refrigerator on its corners. The criticism of this particular theory has always focused on the soft composition of the statue's base, and the fact that this repeated movement would have led to a noticeable rounding of the corners, which consequently would have affected the moai's stability when stood on its ahu. However, this method could have worked well over short distances.

Rolling required the moai to be placed on a wooden sled, either standing vertically or lying horizontally, and the whole structure dragged over wooden rollers in order to reduce the friction with the ground. This particular theory goes some way to explaining how a relatively small population managed to cut down most of the island's trees in such a short period of time, although it was certainly not the only reason for the widespread deforestation.

Irrespective of the method of transportation used, and it may well have been a combination of both techniques depending on the terrain and the phase of transportation, the Rapanui successfully moved over 400 completed statues from Rano Raraku to every single corner of their island. Once the moai arrived at the site where it was to be erected, the next task was to position the statue face-down in front of its ahu and then gradually lift the moai up using long wooden poles as levers. Stones were used to shore up the statue during each stage of the raising process, until it could finally be stood up in a vertical position with the ropes around its head ensuring that the moai didn't topple backwards. At this time, an additional crown or 'topknot' made from red stone was sometimes placed on the head of the statue, adding not only to its overall height but also to the complexity of the masterpiece. Finally, eyes made of white coral were inserted into carved eye sockets in the statue's face, and it was this final act – the only part of the carving process not undertaken in the quarry – that was considered to be the exact moment in which the ancestor's spirit came back to life. With the moai erected at the ancestor's former village and in such a way that it faced inland, so the *mana* of these stone giants was able to offer a protective cloak over all of their descendants.

The statue carving culture on Easter Island lasted for over 500 years and is a fascinating example of the way in which a belief system can develop independently due to a totally isolated environment. Wandering amongst the statues at the abandoned quarry of Rano Raraku today is one of modern travel's most awe-inspiring experiences, as you contemplate hundreds of discarded moai in all stages of carving, the entire site eerily silent ever since workers downed their tools, never to return.

'Rano Raraku remains one of the greatest and most curious creations of mankind, a monument to the great lost unknown behind us...'

- Thor Heyerdahl

Collapse?

There is no doubt that something occurred on Easter Island which prevented these statue carvers from continuing with their activities right up until modern times. We know that a change in the religious belief system had already occurred prior to Roggeveen's arrival in 1722, since he witnessed the statues still standing upright but felt that the islanders no longer possessed any particular connection to them, and he considered them to be remnants of a bygone era. When Captain Cook visited a little over 50 years later, he found the island to be in a noticeably worse state, with many of the statues having been violently thrown from their platforms, and he lamented in his journal: '*No nation will ever contend for the honour of the discovery of this island as there is hardly an island in this sea which affords less refreshments and conveniences for shipping than it does.*'

The key question here is whether this so-called 'collapse' of the Rapanui society was a self-inflicted ecological suicide as suggested by many anthropologists including well-known author Jared Diamond, or whether it was the result of other environmental factors far beyond their control, which ultimately caused this sudden downfall. The population of Easter Island increased exponentially after its settlement and possibly reached as high as 12,000 to 14,000 people by the late 15th century. Living on a remote island with an abundant supply of food and freshwater, together with an absence of any predators, diseases or external threats to their safety, it's not hard to see how the population grew so quickly. However, this peak in the population was soon followed by a sharp decline, with Roggeveen estimating the island to have approximately 6,000 inhabitants when he visited in 1722, while a census performed by the missionaries in 1877 counted just 110.

The islanders' obsession with the production of moai is the most obvious explanation that has been suggested for their rapid demise; the processes of carving and transporting the statues were both extremely labour intensive and required enormous quantities of raw materials, thus putting large pressure on the island's limited resources, particularly its timber. The cutting down of trees began soon after the arrival of the Polynesians as a means of clearing land for agriculture, and the introduction of rats did little to help the palm trees germinate naturally once these rodents got a taste for their seeds. However, recent climatic data for the South Pacific has pointed to a series of intense droughts that affected the island between AD 1500 and 1700, and this lack of rainfall probably led to the extinction of several species of trees, some of which were found only on Easter Island. Roggeveen confirmed in his journal that there was barely any wood on the island with which to light a fire, and that he had initially thought 'Paaseiland' to be covered with sand when he first sighted it, only to discover that it was in fact dry grass. Whatever the explanation, the effects of a fast-growing population, dwindling resources, and an ecology under increasing pressure, forced the islanders to change their way of life almost overnight, including their religious belief systems. The carving of the moai came to an abrupt halt, and the co-operation between tribes which had once been fundamental to their shared success, was soon replaced by internal conflict and the taking of land and resources by the most powerful tribes. In this way, the highly organised, structured society that had once been responsible for creating the largest concentration of archaeology anywhere in the Pacific, descended into inter-tribal warfare and chaos.

The islanders' solution to this turmoil and violence took the form of a unique sporting contest, and one that was conceived without any outside influences or input. Each spring, migratory sooty terns would visit Easter Island in order to nest and raise their chicks, making the arrival of these birds a significant annual event. From the early 18th century onwards, it was decided that each of the island's 12 tribes could appoint one contestant to compete for the first sooty tern egg of that season, with the eventual winner's tribe becoming the dominant clan for the next 12 months. However, the race was no easy task, and involved each competitor scaling

1000-foot cliffs before swimming across 2 miles of open ocean to the offshore islet of Motu Nui, where the unsuspecting sooty terns had built their nests. The contest was effectively over once the first egg had been collected, although the winner did still have to swim back to the main island and present his chief with the intact egg, something he achieved by placing it inside a pouch around his head while he swam and climbed. The competitor's arrival signalled the start of his chief's tenure and greater access to the island's resources for him and his family, before they all came back the following year and held the same race once more!

Known as the 'Birdman competition', this unusual contest served to restore an element of order and stability in an otherwise highly tumultuous period of the island's history, and continued to be employed right up until 1867 when it was finally outlawed by the Catholic missionaries, who objected to the islanders' worshipping of birds' eggs. The significance of the sooty terns seems to have come from the belief that the arrival of these birds was a gift from the gods, and from a place that was far beyond the islanders' reach by then, with the physical egg embodying the *mana* of their divine beings. Once the trees had all disappeared, the Rapanui lost the materials with which to build their oceangoing canoes and sail away from their homeland, effectively marooning themselves on their small island.

When the missionaries first arrived on Easter Island in 1864, they came across an island in an increasingly depleted state and one whose inhabitants were in poor health. Shortly afterwards, an outbreak of tuberculosis wreaked further havoc on this vulnerable population, resulting in the census performed by the church in 1877 that counted just 110 people. The international community eventually woke up to the islanders' predicament, and Chile annexed the island in 1888, having regarded its location as strategically important for its aspirations of expansion. Easter Island remains a part of Chilean territory today, albeit a very distant one, but with a much greater degree of autonomy than it has ever previously enjoyed, and there remains very little interest from either side in complete independence.

One final Easter Island mystery which was unearthed by the missionaries but remains unsolved to this day, was the discovery of numerous wooden tablets covered with an indecipherable script, known as *rongo rongo*. Only 26 original tablets have survived, all of them housed in overseas museums, but you can still appreciate the rows of fine hieroglyphs written in alternating directions and orientations from the previous line, in a writing system known as reverse boustrophedon. Certain linguists have dedicated much of their academic careers to trying to decipher this unique script, but with so few boards having survived and no Rosetta Stone likely to ever be found, this would appear to be one mystery which will endure forever. While some experts have suggested that it may have been nothing more than an elaborate imitation of European handwriting, references to this pictorial writing style are found within the islanders' oral history from before 1722, seemingly confirming that it may have been the only form of writing to have existed anywhere in Polynesia prior to European contact.

Easter Island Today

The clearing of stones from the island's only piece of flat land and the construction of a simple airport finally opened up the island to the rest of the world in 1967, even if it then took over nine hours for the aircraft of that time to cover the approximately 2,500 miles from mainland Chile. When NASA extended the pre-existing runway in order to create an emergency landing site for its space shuttles in 1985, the enlargement of this key facility became the catalyst to Easter Island's tourism industry, with guests initially housed in either tents or very basic guesthouses. There is no doubt that a trip to Easter Island in the late 1980s was definitely more of a wild adventure than any kind of luxury vacation!

Ten years later, the island began receiving several direct flights each week from Santiago de Chile, each one bringing with it the first influx of regular visitors, together with products from the outside world that were previously unavailable. With the introduction of the internet and the speed with which photographs from exotic places could be shared around the world, Easter Island's appeal began to spread, together with the realisation that it was finally possible to visit this remote outpost and marvel at its archaeological wonders for oneself. In fact, tourist numbers to the island began rising at such a fast rate that by 2019 there was even talk of restricting visitor numbers in much the same way as at Machu Picchu and the Galapagos Islands, the region's other two major tourist destinations. Covid-19 ultimately provided the island's inhabitants with the most unexpected reset imaginable, and the island closed its doors for more than 2 years with only very occasional humanitarian flights. The effect on the local economy was obviously cataclysmic, and similar hardships were experienced by nearly all of the other islands in the Pacific, forcing people to return to a subsistence lifestyle that had been replaced more than 30 years ago.

There is a curious irony regarding the moai of Easter Island, given that they were originally carved to bring the islanders prosperity and success, by channelling the *mana* of their deceased ancestors into their present lives. While it worked for a long time, this belief system ultimately came crashing down together with the statues several centuries later. However, with the current boom in the island's tourism industry and visitors flying in from all over the world to marvel at the archaeology, the moai are once again providing their descendants with enormous economic benefits - just not in the manner that their ancestors could have ever envisioned, and much later than the original carvers had planned for!

7. The Final Flight of Amelia Earhart

'Please know I am quite aware of the hazards. I want to do it because I want to do it. Women must try to do things as men have tried. When they fail, their failure must be but a challenge to others.'

– Amelia Earhart

There are few people whose adventurous spirit has appealed to the American public in quite the same way as that of Amelia Earhart, a woman far ahead of her time both as an aviator and as a pioneer of gender equality. Her rise to global fame began with her extraordinary accomplishments as a pilot, but there is a sense that if she had lived longer, then the furthering of the women's liberation movement would have become an even more prominent part of her later life, and that she would have served as an inspiration to even more young women today.

Amelia Mary Earhart was born in Atchison, Kansas in 1897 and spent most of her childhood with her maternal grandparents and younger sister, Muriel. Her parents had moved to Kansas City for her father's work, before he was finally able to secure a job in Iowa and reunite their family once more. Amelia grew up enjoying hobbies that were usually associated with the opposite sex, such as American football, baseball, and even hunting rats with a .22 rifle and was therefore seen as a classic tomboy. It was at the Iowa State Fair in 1908 where Amelia caught sight of her first aeroplane, although it made little impression on the 11-year-old, who was much more enthusiastic about her studies at school, particularly the sciences.

While staying with her sister in Toronto during the First World War, Amelia was inspired to join the war effort and soon found herself training as a volunteer nurse's aide, where she had her first close contact with injured pilots. However, it wasn't until she attended an air show in Long Beach, California in 1920 that she had the opportunity to take her first ride in an aeroplane, and by the time the ten-minute introductory flight was over, she knew that she'd found her vocation. She began taking flying lessons the following year and paid for them by doing a mix of odd jobs, including working as a shorthand typist and even as a truck driver. She obtained her American pilot's licence in December 1921 and her international license two years later, becoming only the 16th woman in the U.S. to hold such a qualification.

Public interest in aviation was at its peak following the first ever solo crossing of the Atlantic Ocean by Charles Lindbergh on 20th May 1927, and the idea of a woman crossing the same ocean by aeroplane was proposed shortly after. George Putnam, a literary agent who had been responsible for the publication of Lindbergh's autobiography, *We*, believed that the story of a female pilot had all the makings of another best-seller, and he contacted Amelia who accepted his offer immediately. While she was listed on the flight's manifest as a crewmember, she was never permitted to take the controls during the successful crossing between Newfoundland and Wales, since it was all flown under instrument flight rules (IFR) and she wasn't yet qualified for that type of flying. Nevertheless, she gained enormous notoriety from the adventure and wrote her first book about the experience, *20 Hours 40 Minutes*, which Putnam duly published on her behalf. On their return to the United States, the crew were all welcomed back as heroes, later enjoying a ticker-tape parade along Manhattan and a personal audience with President Calvin Coolidge.

In the following years, Earhart achieved a series of aviation 'firsts' for both men and women by breaking records in altitude, speed, and distance, as well as winning numerous flying races across the country. She completed an extensive lecture tour of the U.S. and became the face of various well-known brands, from luggage to cigarettes, and she even launched her own clothing line. She also married George Putnam at the sixth time of his asking, although she was quite clear about their future relationship: *'On our life together I want you to understand I shall not hold you to any midaevil [sic] code of faithfulness to me nor shall I consider myself bound to you similarly. ... In this connection I may have to keep some place where I can go to be myself, now and then, for I cannot guarantee to endure at all times the confinements of even an attractive cage.'* Quite the prenup indeed, and she also refused to take his surname, preferring instead to keep her maiden name for the rest of her life.

Her most prestigious feat in aviation came on 20th May 1932, exactly five years to the day since Charles Lindbergh's momentous flight. She took off from Harbour Grace in Newfoundland with a copy of the local newspaper in order to corroborate her departure date, but only told very few people of her actual intentions. She planned to mirror Lindbergh's same flight route and land in France, but after almost 15 hours of battling strong headwinds, icy conditions, and various mechanical issues, she put her Lockheed Vega 5B down not in the centre of Paris but in Robert Gallagher's cow field in Derry, Northern Ireland. In doing so, she became the first woman to fly solo non-stop across the Atlantic, and when the confused farmer found her and asked if she'd flown far, she simply replied 'From America'.

She was presented with numerous awards for her brave achievement, including the Distinguished Flying Cross from the U.S. Government, becoming the first woman to ever receive this honour. Her new-found celebrity status led to a close friendship with First Lady Eleanor Roosevelt, who was also a prominent activist for women's rights at that time. Following her successful flight across the Atlantic, Earhart continued to break long-distance flying records, becoming the first woman to fly non-stop across the United States and from Mexico City to New York, as well as the first man or woman ever to fly between Hawai'i and the U.S. mainland. However, there was one remaining aviation record that still intrigued her, namely to become the first person to circumnavigate the globe via an equatorial route. For this venture she would need a new, larger aircraft with a greater range and increased reliability, and she eventually raised the funds to replace her trusty single-engine Vega with a twin-engine Lockheed 10E Electra.

Around The World Flight

The planning for an endeavour of this magnitude took many months, since no one had ever attempted to fly the 29,000-mile circumnavigation with just a single aeroplane, and the journey included a complete transpacific crossing, which was still a formidable proposition in a piston-powered aircraft. Before her departure, Earhart needed to obtain countless landing permissions and arrange for spare aircraft parts to be shipped all over the world, including two brand-new engines which were sent to Pakistan for refitting there. She also had to plan a route that offered the best chances of favourable weather conditions, and the direction of travel was chosen to avoid coinciding with the worst of the monsoon season in South Asia. As for the navigation, all of Earhart's previous long-distance flights had involved flying towards continents, and therefore the consequences of any errors in her dead-reckoning navigation had generally been insignificant. On this occasion however, pinpointing tiny islands in the middle of an enormous ocean was going to require the most precise navigational techniques, and Earhart took an additional course in celestial navigation especially for this expedition.

While Earhart was used to always flying alone, attempting to fly the transpacific legs by herself would have been foolhardy, and so she assembled the best possible crew available: the stunt pilot Paul Mantz, who helped her prepare the aircraft and would assist with flying duties as far as Hawai'i, together with the navy sea captain Harry Manning as her navigator for the technical over-water legs as far as Australia. Amelia's husband insisted that she also take Fred Noonan as an additional navigator for the first two sectors, since it was believed that he had more experience than Manning, and he had previously worked for Pan Am and participated in numerous Pacific Ocean crossings. Once they arrived in Australia, she would fly the rest of the trip alone.

Crossing the Pacific Ocean has always been regarded as something of a final frontier in endurance travel, whether by aeroplane (first achieved by Charles Kingsford Smith in 1928), solo in a hot air balloon (Steve Fossett in 1995), or non-stop in a rowing boat, achieved in 1983 by Peter Bird after 294 days alone at sea. Thirteen years later, Bird would attempt to row the same journey again but this time from west to east, only to disappear two months after his departure from Russia, never to be seen again. In the case of Amelia Earhart, she was adamant that her reasons for undertaking this endeavour were not for any particular record but rather for the excitement of a new adventure, to improve her piloting skills, and to inspire young women to face challenges which were usually only reserved for men: *'There was my belief that now and then women should do for themselves what men have already done – and occasionally what men have not done – thereby establishing themselves as persons, and perhaps encouraging other women toward greater independence of thought and action.'*

Earhart also saw the flight as a wide-ranging scientific experiment and fondly referred to the Electra as her 'flying laboratory'. While her aircraft would be tested to its limits during the course of the circumnavigation, she was equally interested in studying the effects that the flight would have on the human body. She was, once again, far ahead of her time in questioning the sacrifice of pilot comfort for increased speed and range in aeroplanes, and she intended to use the next six weeks as an opportunity for performing a number of different trials. She hoped to study the ways in which altitude affected metabolism and discover the kind of nutrition that was most beneficial to flying, as well as the effects of diet on a pilot's fatigue levels. The cockpit of her Electra was noticeably more complex than that of her Vega, and she was keen to test the ways in which more developed aircraft also contributed to a pilot's fatigue.

On the afternoon of 17th March 1937, the crew departed on the first leg of their global circumnavigation from Oakland, California to Honolulu, Hawai'i. The flight itself was long and uneventful but required a continuous and concerted effort from each crew member, something which surprised Earhart who had been expecting a lighter workload during the first few legs. The Electra performed faultlessly, and their navigation was equally precise, providing them with the reassuring sight of Diamond Head after 2,400 miles of open ocean and nearly 16 hours of flying. The original plan had been to refuel the aircraft and continue straight on to Howland Island, but bad weather meant they had to spend a few days waiting in Honolulu, something which proved to be no great sacrifice for any of the crew! Paul Mantz left the expedition at this point, as he had also been using the flight to hitch a ride to Hawai'i, where his fiancée was waiting for him.

The second leg of the journey was to be from Hawai'i to the uninhabited U.S. territory of Howland Island, where the Americans had built an unpaved runway in order to establish a refuelling stop for transpacific flights. Howland is a remote island in the South Pacific nearly 2,000 miles southwest of Hawai'i, with a land area of barely one square mile. Surrounded by nothing but ocean, it would require perfect navigation by Manning and Noonan all along the route to pinpoint such a minuscule target. However, on this occasion the Electra never even left the ground in Hawai'i; during the take-off run on the wet runway at Luke Field, a suspected tyre-burst meant that Earhart lost control of the aircraft and ended up with all of the plane's weight on the right landing gear, causing the strut to collapse. The aircraft's two propellers both struck the ground, and the Electra spun on the tarmac in a shower of sparks and dust. None of the crew were seriously injured, but the aircraft was badly damaged, and the only option was to ship the plane back to California by sea and hope that it could be repaired. Inconsolable after her around-the-world attempt had been curtailed after only the first leg, Earhart left for the mainland that same afternoon by steamship.

Three months later and with the repairs to the Electra having been completed, Earhart had lost none of her determination to try for the same world record once again. For this second attempt she would take only Fred Noonan with her as her navigator and companion, and the pair would fly in the opposite direction, leaving the transpacific leg for the very end. This change of route required a whole new series of flight plans, with much of the focus again on avoiding the monsoon in India, and many of the preparations that had been made for the first attempt now had to be redone from scratch. On 1st June 1937, Earhart and Noonan took off from Oakland Airport bound for Miami, very much as a shakedown flight after the extensive repairs that had been done to the aircraft. Although they could have flown directly between the two cities, they stopped off in Burbank, Tucson, and New Orleans along the way, so that newspaper stories could be written about the pair in each location, providing valuable publicity for their record attempt. Amelia was already an established aviation celebrity, and was well aware of the benefits of a good relationship with the press.

After arriving safely in Miami, Earhart was still not satisfied with all of the repairs that had been made to the Electra, and they spent a further week in Florida overseeing additional adjustments, in particular to the navigational equipment and radios. From Miami they flew south to Puerto Rico, and from there they continued to Venezuela, Suriname, and Brazil. This was followed by one of the most challenging legs, the transatlantic flight from Northeast Brazil to Senegal, crossing almost 2,000 miles of open ocean in potentially turbulent conditions close to the equator. In Senegal, they didn't actually arrive at their intended destination of Dakar, and instead crossed the coastline 100 miles to the north, forcing them to land at Saint-Louis airport instead. A relatively minor error perhaps, but a very significant miscalculation in the context of their next transoceanic crossing.

Earhart flew one sector per day where possible, and in the month of June alone she flew a total of 25 legs, taking the pair all the way from Florida to Papua New Guinea. The days when she was unable to fly were generally due to bad weather, and she only ever awarded herself a day off after a particularly gruelling leg the day before. They arrived in Lae, the second largest city in Papua New Guinea, on 29th June 1937, where they spent several days waiting for the weather conditions along their planned route to improve and also preparing the Electra for the final three sectors across the Pacific Ocean. Only 7,000 miles now lay between them and Oakland, and Amelia Earhart had already telephoned her husband from Java confirming her intention to land back on the U.S. mainland in time for the 4th of July celebrations. There have been suggestions that Earhart's desire to complete her global circumnavigation by this significant date may have caused the pair to hurry their final preparations in Lae, but no evidence of any corners having been cut has ever been found. However, rumours have persisted surrounding Earhart's health by this stage of the journey and that she may well have been suffering from exhaustion, while Noonan was possibly drinking heavily too, although neither allegation has ever been substantiated.

At 10am on 2nd July 1937, with the tanks of the Lockheed Electra filled up with 1,100 gallons of gasoline (well over the factory-recommended maximum), Earhart took off on the 2,556-mile run from Papua New Guinea to Howland Island, and the second time that she would attempt to reach that island. The flight was expected to last approximately 18½ hours, making it the longest leg of the whole trip, and they were carrying enough fuel in reserve for an additional four hours of flying. An eyewitness on the ground noted that the plane struggled to get airborne before the end of the runway, confirming that it was extremely heavily loaded with fuel. Unfortunately, there was one significant detail that the eyewitness failed to notice, which was only picked up by subsequent studies of grainy photographs and film, namely that the antenna wire which ran along the belly of the aircraft had broken off at some point during the bumpy taxi out to the runway. The cable was definitely attached when they boarded the aircraft before the flight, but no longer connected by the time that the plane took off, and this would be a significant factor in the failed two-way communications later on in the journey.

Since this particular flight path had never been flown before, the United States Government provided important logistical support in the form of two U.S. Navy ships placed at strategic points along the route: USS *Ontario* was positioned at the halfway point between Lae and Howland Island, and USCGC *Itasca* was anchored next to Howland, ready to guide the Electra in. It is unclear whether Earhart and Noonan ever spotted the *Ontario* at the midway point, but it seems unlikely since the ship's crew never saw or heard the Electra, and in the past Earhart had always flown over any ships at low altitude, in the hope that they would radio the authorities and confirm her exact position. Furthermore, the *Ontario* and Earhart never managed to successfully communicate with each other, since the *Ontario* was operating a 'LF' (low frequency) radio, while the Electra was now carrying only a 'HF' (high frequency) model.

The sun rose over Howland Island on 3rd July 1937 under overcast skies, and weather reports from nearby islands suggested that much of Earhart's flight had also taken place under cloudy conditions, making it extremely difficult for Noonan to have taken any celestial readings along the route. Without this navigational aid, the pair were relying solely on dead reckoning, a formula based on the speed of the aeroplane, the distance flown, and the speed and direction of the winds surrounding them. A mistake in calculating any one of these values could put them dangerously off course in a flight of this length, and there were no visual landmarks in the vast ocean to help guide them. Their aim was to get within range of the *Itasca* in order to pick up a compass bearing from the ship, at which point the navigators on board could guide the aeroplane towards the island and subsequently the airfield.

The radio operators on board the *Itasca* were able to hear most of Earhart's transmissions as the aircraft neared its destination, but their responses were seemingly never picked up by the Electra. Earhart was also never able to establish a directional bearing towards the *Itasca* as they approached, suggesting that they weren't in fact as close to the island as they thought, and effectively leaving them flying blind over the ocean. As with the *Ontario*, the *Itasca* was transmitting on a different type of radio than the Electra, and consistent two-way radio communications between the two parties were never established. Ironically, Earhart had requested that an additional antenna, known as a trailing wire antenna, which could be unwound and dangled beneath the aircraft, be removed from the aeroplane in Miami due to weight concerns, and this emergency antenna would have allowed her to transmit using the 500-kilocycle marine frequency which the *Itasca* was also tuned into.

By now Earhart had descended to just 1,000 feet and was trying desperately to locate either the island or the U.S. Coast Guard ship. Believing they were now at the correct longitude for Howland, they decided to fly north and south along a 157°/337° bearing, in the hope that either one of their targets would soon appear in front of them. They had been flying for over 20 hours by now, well beyond the anticipated duration of their flight, and close to the limits of their remaining fuel. The final radio transmissions from Earhart to the *Itasca* display a continued professionalism under increasingly desperate circumstances:

07.42 LT 'We must be on you but cannot see you … but gas is running low. Have been unable to reach you by radio. We are flying at 1,000 feet.'

07.50 LT 'We are circling but cannot hear you.'

08.43 LT 'On the line 157 337 … running north and south. We will repeat this message. We will repeat this on 6210 kilocycles. Wait.'

It is unclear how close they ever actually flew to Howland Island, but these were the final transmissions from the Electra received by the *Itasca*. Prior to leaving Papua New Guinea, a contingency plan had been agreed upon that if Earhart failed to sight Howland, she would fly back due west to the Gilbert Islands (modern-day Kiribati) and try to land there. Despite the lack of any formal airstrips in the whole of the island chain, its friendly government and welcoming inhabitants were seen as the best option in an otherwise desolate corner of the Pacific. The only other alternatives were the Phoenix Islands to the south of Howland, or the Marshall Islands to the north; however, the former were completely uninhabited, while the latter were already under Japanese occupation in 1937 and would therefore not welcome two U.S. citizens. Ultimately, the contingency plan was never activated, and no aircraft ever landed in the Gilbert Islands that day. After several more hours of radio silence, the crew of the *Itasca* assumed that they had run out of fuel and ditched in the ocean, and began a frantic search of the surrounding area. For the next two weeks, a search and rescue operation of unprecedented scale involving the U.S. Navy and Coast Guard, and even the Japanese Navy, scoured some 250,000 square miles of ocean, but no traces of either Earhart, Noonan, or their Electra were ever found. The search was called off after 16 days, however Earhart's husband continued to fund his own private search operation for three more months, until in January 1939, 18 months after her disappearance, a U.S. court order declared Earhart officially dead. She would have been 41 years old.

Possible Theories

No confirmed wreckage of the Lockheed Electra has ever been found, nor any human remains conclusively proven to have belonged to either Amelia Earhart or Fred Noonan. Trying to solve the events of this final flight has been a life's work for many researchers and aviation historians, but even after nearly a century there have been no significant breakthroughs.

Given the lack of any physical evidence after so many exhaustive searches, the most logical explanation, and the one shared by the U.S. Navy, is that the aircraft ran out of fuel and crashed into the sea, where it broke up and sank. Known as the crash-and-sink theory, it would certainly explain the lack of wreckage and why no traces of either crewmember have ever been found. The *Itasca* was the only ship in the vicinity able to carry out an immediate search, and even her crew didn't know in which direction they should be looking; it took several more days for any other vessels to arrive at the search area, by which time the aircraft would have almost certainly sunk together with its occupants.

Alternatively, The International Group for Historic Aircraft Recovery (TIGHAR, pronounced 'Tiger'), who have organised many of the expeditions to search for Earhart, believe there are simply too many individual pieces of evidence supporting the theory that the crew survived, albeit possibly only for a short time. According to their investigations, numerous amateur radio operators heard a woman's voice repeatedly requesting for help on the day of their disappearance, suggesting that the pair might have survived a crash-landing and that their communications equipment was still working. This leads to the question, if Earhart didn't land on Howland Island or in the surrounding sea, then where could she have put the Electra down? From the final radio broadcast, we know that she was following the 157°/337° compass heading either to or from Howland, which has led investigators to examine the other islands that also lie on that line. One of them, a small coral atoll called Gardner Island, is where archaeologists from TIGHAR believe that Earhart and Noonan landed that day. The island has been uninhabited since 1892, but the U.S. Navy planes that overflew the island one week after the Electra vanished apparently noticed signs of recent habitation. Three years after their disappearance, a partial skeleton was discovered on Gardner Island, and although it was initially concluded to have belonged to a man, subsequent studies of the report (but not of the bones) suggest that they could also have belonged to a woman of about 5' 7", the same height as Earhart. A radio message picked up in Texas on the day of disappearance apparently reported *'Plane down on an uncharted island. Small, uninhabited ... partially on land, part in water'*, and suggested that both crewmembers were seriously injured, without identifying who they were. However, many experts doubt that the radio equipment on board the Electra would have been capable of transmitting further than a few hundred miles, and numerous searches of Gardner Island have failed to unearth any evidence of recent human activity there. Nevertheless, a few interesting artefacts that could date from Earhart's era have been found on the island, including the sole of a woman's shoe, a piece of aluminium with rivets that possibly came from an aircraft, and a jar of freckle ointment which Earhart was known to use. Earhart and Noonan could have survived on Gardner for a number of days, but with no freshwater and limited food, as well as both perhaps being badly injured, their chances of surviving there as castaways for an extended period of time would have been very small. The bones that were examined in 1940 have sadly since been lost, and therefore cannot be re-examined using modern DNA techniques.

Most of the other hypotheses concerning the fate of Earhart and Noonan descend into the realm of fantasy and conspiracy theories, and have little or no scientific evidence to support them. For a while, people believed that the pair might have been captured and killed by the Japanese, while others have suggested that the whole expedition was in fact a guise for espionage by the U.S. Government. Sightings of the two were reported as far away as the Marshall Islands, and in the case of Earhart, even back in New Jersey!

Without the discovery of either the wreckage of the Electra or a DNA match of either crewmember, the mystery surrounding the final flight of Amelia Earhart will probably remain unsolved forever. It is worth remembering just how difficult finding a small object in the ocean can be, as the search for the *Titanic* and Malaysia Airlines flight 370 have already demonstrated. In the case of *Titanic*, experts knew the approximate location of the wreck, and despite measuring 880 feet long, it still took 73 years for the ship to be found. For MH370 the search area is much less clear, but state-of-the-art sonar equipment has so far been unable to detect the Boeing 777, with almost no expense having been spared. The task for anyone trying to locate Amelia Earhart's Lockheed 10E Electra today is by no means an easy one, and it will require considerable time, money, and good fortune to find it.

Legacy

Far beyond being an extraordinary aviator in her own right, Earhart was well ahead of her time in questioning gender roles and bringing attention to the discrimination and challenges facing female students, particularly those at Purdue University in Indiana, where she was a faculty member: *'The problems and opportunities of these girls were quite as much my concern as aviation matters ... often youngsters are sadly miscast. I have known girls who should be tinkering with mechanical things instead of making dresses, and boys who would do better at cooking than engineering.'* She was also a founding member and the first president of the Ninety-Nines, an organisation created to encourage more women pilots, which today has become an international organisation with thousands of members worldwide.

There is a poignancy to the fact that Earhart planned to retire from long-distance flying after the completion of her around-the-world voyage and dedicate herself to lecturing and instructing instead, although she insisted that she would never give up flying altogether. The Lockheed Vega that she flew across the Atlantic is now preserved at the National Air & Space Museum in Washington D.C., and a museum devoted to her life recently opened near to her birthplace in Kansas, with the centrepiece being the world's last remaining Lockheed 10E Electra. Whether the mystery of her disappearance is ultimately ever solved is probably of lesser importance today; with most airlines now actively recruiting female pilots and it no longer unusual to take a flight with an all-female flight crew, the true legacy of Amelia Earhart's heroic life is unquestionably alive and well in our modern society.

Courage

Courage is the price that Life exacts for granting peace,
The soul that knows it not, knows no release,
From little things;

Knows not the livid loneliness of fear
Nor mountain heights where bitter joy can hear
The sound of wings.

- Amelia Earhart

8. Robert Louis Stevenson: from Scotland to Samoa

'The first experience can never be repeated. The first love, the first sunrise, the first South Sea Island are memories apart and touched by a virginity of sense.'

– Robert Louis Stevenson

People are often surprised that so little is known about one of Scotland's most successful engineering companies – the one that built nearly every single lighthouse in the country – due to its family name having been completely outshone by the literary achievements of one of its descendants. Robert Stevenson (1772–1850) and his three sons, Alan, David, and Thomas, were responsible for the construction of nearly all of Scotland's lighthouses, and it is therefore no exaggeration to say that they literally illuminated the entire Scottish coastline during the 19th century. Many of these projects were done in the most challenging of locations, none more so than the Bell Rock lighthouse, situated in the middle of the North Sea some 11 miles from the coast, on a large rock that is fully submerged except at low tide. After countless shipwrecks had been caused by this hidden outcrop, it was agreed that a lighthouse should be built there, and the contract given to Robert Stevenson. It took three years for him to complete the structure, and although the light has been automated since 1988, the Bell Rock Lighthouse is still considered to be one of the Seven Wonders of the Industrial World today.

Thomas Stevenson, the youngest of Robert's three sons, had also followed in his father's footsteps and become a skilled civil engineer, designing over 30 of Scotland's lighthouses himself, most of which are still in service today. In 1848 he married Margaret Balfour, and two years later she gave birth to their only child, a son who they christened Robert Lewis Balfour Stevenson. As a young adult, Robert would change the spelling of Lewis to Louis, and drop the name Balfour altogether, creating the name Robert Louis Stevenson (RLS) by which the world knows him today.

RLS was a thin and sickly child, slightly odd-looking and prone to coughs and fevers from an early age. While growing up he continued to be afflicted by his bad lungs, greatly affecting his ability to attend school in person and resulting in his being home-schooled by private tutors for most of his childhood. He was briefly sent away to boarding school in England, where his health improved sufficiently for him to be able to attend a school in Edinburgh from the age of 14, at the end of which he was offered a place at Edinburgh University to study engineering. His father was sure that he would follow in the family business of lighthouse construction and he took his son to all corners of Scotland during the summer holidays in order to inspect the family's creations. Beyond the excitement that RLS felt for discovering new places, he also wrote with great pride about the legacies of his close family:

'There is scarce a deep sea light from the Isle of
Man to North Berwick,
but one of my blood designed it.
The Bell Rock stands monument for my grandfather;
the Skerryvore for my uncle Alan;
and when the lights come out along the shores of Scotland,
I am proud to think that they burn more brightly for the genius of
my father.'

However, despite this delight that he felt for his ancestors' achievements, RLS felt no vocation whatsoever towards his own engineering studies and regularly skipped lectures, preferring instead to spend time in drama classes and debating circles. It probably came as no surprise to his father when, at the age of 21, RLS announced that he would not be following in the footsteps of the other Stevensons and intended to become a writer instead. In a bid to have him study *something*, Thomas Stevenson persuaded his son to read law at Edinburgh University, with a view to him being called to the Scottish Bar. By this point RLS was rebelling even further against the norms of his family's social circle by letting his hair grow long, wearing bohemian clothes such as his trademark velvet jackets, and most shockingly of all perhaps for that period, declaring himself an atheist. This final announcement caused deep anguish to his parents, both devout Presbyterians themselves, and a sense that they had failed in their duties of raising their only son. RLS continued to suffer from ill health while he was at university and took to travelling overseas during the holidays in the hope of finding an environment which would be more beneficial to his weak lungs. He visited the French Riviera and also spent some time in Paris, at a time when the bohemian lifestyle was in full swing. It was perhaps something of a surprise, therefore, when he managed to qualify for the Scottish Bar at the age of 25, and even though he ultimately never once practised as a barrister, his father was sufficiently proud of his son's achievements to have a brass plate added to the outside of their family home that read: *R.L. Stevenson, Advocate.*

At this stage of his life, RLS's two passions were literature and travel, and it was while he was on a writing trip through Europe that he first met the woman who would later become his wife, Fanny Van de Grift Osbourne. She was American, separated from her husband, and the mother of three young children; she was also about ten years older than RLS. They spent a happy year together in France, but Fanny later returned to America and seemingly back into the arms of her estranged husband, and she and RLS wouldn't become an official couple for another two years. The family and friends of RLS were deeply concerned to see him so smitten with a woman who they regarded as completely unsuitable, and they watched with increasing despair as RLS followed her across the Atlantic, choosing to traverse the entire continent by train in order to give himself more writing material for his next book. Ultimately, the transatlantic voyage and subsequent train journey nearly killed him, and he only managed to get as far as Monterey, California before the effects of a pulmonary haemorrhage forced him to check himself into a hotel and spend the next four months recovering. By this point, Fanny's marriage had ended for good, and she dutifully nursed RLS back to some form of good health, while he finally convinced her to file for legal separation from her husband. With her divorce complete, the couple were free to marry in 1880, despite RLS still being in the early stages of his writing career and having almost no money to his name. His health also remained in a precarious state, and on his wedding day he was, by his own admission, '*a mere complication of cough and bones, much fitter for an emblem of mortality than a bridegroom*'. Their honeymoon was spent in the Napa Valley region, together with Fanny's eldest son Lloyd, and the trip is the focus for RLS's book *The Silverado Squatters*, published in 1883.

The new family spent those first few years together travelling between America and Britain, before finally settling in Bournemouth, a large town on the south coast of England. During the 18th and 19th centuries, it was believed that nearly all ailments, from tuberculosis to depression, could be cured by sea air, and yet RLS ultimately spent most of the next three years bedridden. Nonetheless, this period turned out to be one of the most productive for his writing, and here in the south of England he wrote some of his most successful and enduring works: *Treasure Island* (1883), *A Child's Garden of Verses* (1885), *Kidnapped* (1886), and *Strange Case of Dr Jekyll and Mr Hyde* (1886).

While they were still living in Bournemouth, news arrived from Scotland that Thomas Stevenson was gravely ill, and RLS and Fanny rushed north to be at his bedside. They unfortunately arrived too late for RLS to have any meaningful dialogue with his father, and he died soon after. Unbeknownst to RLS, this was to be the last time that he would ever set foot in Scotland, and the death of his father seemingly removed any obligation for him to continue living in Britain and also gave him the freedom to pursue some of his more unorthodox projects. He received a healthy inheritance from his father's estate which at last allowed him financial independence, and he was also given official medical advice recommending that he move overseas to somewhere with a drier climate. The family initially considered moving to Colorado, but eventually chose Saranac Lake in upstate New York, where the air was believed to be especially beneficial for those suffering from pulmonary disease. His recently widowed mother, Margaret Stevenson, now affectionately referred to as Aunt Maggie, also joined them in North America, although the sub-zero temperatures in winter soon had them reaching for their maps once again and searching for warmer climes. They considered various islands in the Indian Ocean as well as the Mediterranean, including Madeira, but it was the direct influence of the American author Charles Warren Stoddard, who had written extensively about the South Pacific and about Polynesian culture, who suggested they take a voyage to the South Sea Islands instead. RLS was enthusiastic about the journey in his own self-effacing style: '*For nearly ten years my health had been declining; and for some while before I set forth upon my voyage, I believed I was coming to the afterpiece of life, and had only the nurse and undertaker to expect. It was suggested that I should try the South Seas; and I was not unwilling to visit like a ghost, and be carried like a bale, among scenes that had attracted me in youth and health.*'

The family had no intention of settling in the Pacific, but travelling to its far-flung islands had been a dream of RLS's from a young age, and his fascination with exotic travel was no doubt an inspiration for the Jim Hawkins character in *Treasure Island*. Had it not been for his poor health, RLS would probably have spent as much of his life exploring as he did writing, and it is no surprise that all of his early works were travel books. Fanny was sent from New York to San Francisco with the task of finding a yacht to charter, and she wrote back to say that she had been offered an elegant, two-masted schooner with space for 12 people on board, named the *Casco*.

The travelling party of RLS, Fanny, Fanny's son Lloyd Osbourne, Aunt Maggie, and their Swiss maid, together with the ship's crew of six, departed for the Marquesas Islands in June 1888, and the effect on RLS's health and spirits was almost immediate. Time on board was spent reading and writing, while in the evenings the party would gather in the ship's sitting room to play several hands of whist. Prior to their departure, an American publisher had given RLS the down payment for a book and various essays to be written during the voyage, and so he was even more financially comfortable and able to enjoy the voyage to the full. '*In health, spirits, renewed interest in life, and, I do believe, refreshed capacity for work, the cruise has proved a wise folly*', he wrote from the *Casco*, as they island-hopped their way across the Pacific, visiting the Marquesas, Tuamotus, Society Islands, and Hawai'i. Fanny, on the other hand, suffered terribly from seasickness, and seems to have undertaken this voyage entirely for the well-being of her husband.

RLS found the islanders that he encountered along the way to be charming and friendly, and when they arrived in Hawai'i and the *Casco* was required in San Francisco, the family decided to stay in the islands and continue their sojourn in Polynesia. Soon after, Aunt Maggie decided to leave the voyage and make her own way back to Edinburgh. Margaret Stevenson was a formidable woman who had thrown off the shackles of her aristocratic lifestyle after she had been widowed, and she embraced the South Pacific in a manner that would have appeared unrecognisable to her friends back in Victorian Scotland. She dressed in the same brightly coloured dresses worn by the women in Polynesia and took the opportunity to walk barefoot in the sand whenever she could. During that Pacific journey she blossomed into an increasingly independent and free-spirited woman, and she also acted as an important counterbalance in the relationship between Fanny and her son.

The rest of the family spent the next five months in Hawai'i, where they became closely acquainted with the Hawaiian royal family, while RLS took a deep interest in Polynesian culture. He didn't particularly like Honolulu, and he was disappointed to see the 'American Dream' usurping the island's traditional way of life, and bemoaned the introduction of cars and telephones into the local culture. However, this period also awoke in him an avid interest in the politics of the region, and particularly the effects of the colonial administrations in these islands after having seen similar attitudes by the French in Tahiti. He was also greatly enjoying being a temporary resident somewhere as opposed to a wandering traveller, and during this extended stay he was able to appreciate and empathise much more with the plight of the indigenous islanders.

When the Stevenson family decided that it was finally time to leave, they booked passages on the *Equator*, a trading schooner that followed a published itinerary as opposed to a private charter such as the *Casco* had been. This meant that the passengers went wherever the ship needed to go, in this case mainly on runs around the islands of Micronesia in the western Pacific. RLS and his family spent extensive time in the Gilbert Islands (modern-day Kiribati), before the ship eventually called in at Upolu, the main island of the Samoan archipelago. It was here that their plans, and ultimately the rest of RLS's life, changed forever.

Samoa

Neither RLS nor Fanny had ever intended to settle anywhere during this voyage, but rather to complete their trip in the Pacific and return home to Bournemouth, despite the apathy felt by RLS towards the south coast of England. Neither were he nor Fanny particularly smitten by Upolu initially – it is by no means the prettiest island in Polynesia – but this all changed when they met Harry J. Moors, an American trader who had already been living there for five years. The exact reasons for their decision remain unknown, but within a few days of their arrival the Stevensons had decided to make Samoa their home, and with the help of Moors they purchased 314 acres of fertile land a few miles south of the capital, Apia. There they began the construction of a sizeable mansion – the first two-storey building in Samoa at that time – which was to be called Villa Vailima, located just outside the small village of Vailima. However, with nowhere to live while their new house was being built, they decided to continue with their travels on board the *Equator* and left the project in the safe hands of Harry Moors, while they in turn set sail for Australia.

In Sydney RLS again suffered one of his recurring lung haemorrhages, and this one appears to have been almost fatal. Fanny realised that her husband's health would be best served by a return to the open sea, and so they joined their third ship, the *Janet Nicoll*, as fare-paying passengers on its services around the Marshall Islands, New Caledonia, and Samoa. They used the occasional stops in Apia to check up on the progress of their house, until in September 1890 they disembarked the ship in Samoa for the last time, bringing an end to more than two years of Pacific travels. RLS now accepted that his health would never allow him to live the nomadic lifestyle that he'd once dreamed of, and so he gave instructions for their house in Bournemouth to be sold and most of their furniture to be shipped out to Samoa. He also invited his mother to come and live with them at Villa Vailima, showing not only his deep affection for her, but also perhaps his need to have his mother close by. The pluck and resilience of Aunt Maggie was reconfirmed once more, as she gave up her comfortable lifestyle in Edinburgh's New Town and relocated to the other side of the world, and to a Pacific Island that she'd never even visited before.

The word 'home' had never featured prominently in the vocabulary of RLS and Fanny, and even during their years spent living in San Francisco, Bournemouth, or New York, there was always a sense of transience. However, in Villa Vailima they had at last made a home for themselves, and RLS set to work studying as much as he possibly could about the local politics and learning the Samoan language. He didn't find the Samoans particularly easy people to live amongst and found their casual attitudes towards both work and honesty extremely frustrating; however, he admired their culture for the alternative that it offered to western society, and he did eventually develop a profound respect for the island and its people.

One advantage that Samoa offered over other Pacific Islands was that it was a scheduled stop for steamers sailing between California and Australia, providing RLS with access to a regular mail service. In this way, he was able to send his writings to his publisher, correspond regularly with friends from all over the world, and even have letters published in *The Times* and other international newspapers. As soon as a ship docked in Apia Harbour, he would have his mail rushed to him, at which point he would do little else except read his correspondence and write his replies; his letters would then be hurried back to the wharf where they would depart on the same ship.

RLS settled into a daily work routine in Samoa that maintained a consistently high literary output throughout his time there. He rose early to begin his writing before the rest of the house had stirred, and wrote solidly from 6am to 10.30. Lunch was taken at 11am, after which he dedicated his afternoons to leisure, either bathing in one of the nearby freshwater pools, playing music, gardening, or riding his horse, Jack. The family usually all played cards together in the evenings, and at least once a week they would either entertain guests at home or go out, often involving dancing, which RLS greatly enjoyed. For the Samoans, the author remained something of an enigma, as they never saw him doing any physical work, and he appeared to spend large parts of his day relaxing. Furthermore, they saw him living a comparatively affluent life with a steady stream of income, and with an almost non-existent literary scene in Samoa at the end of the 19th century, it was a mystery to them how he paid for it all. Polynesians love to give each other nicknames, although it was in fact a European missionary who named RLS '*Tusitala*' (literally 'the writer of tales'), and the name stuck with him throughout his time in Samoa.

RLS was also unusual amongst the expat community for taking a genuine interest in the plight of the Samoans, and he concerned himself with local politics in a way that most outsiders generally did not. This isolated him to some degree from the other foreign residents but endeared him enormously to the Samoans. While he could have stayed within the comfortable surroundings of Villa Vailima and dedicated himself entirely to his writing, he instead chose to be an occasionally vociferous critic of what he saw around him, whether it was the unscrupulous behaviour of foreign businessmen, or even of the Samoan government itself. This led to him living under the constant threat of deportation for inciting public disorder, although RLS instead saw himself as an impartial peacekeeper trying to prevent the conflicting Samoan factions from descending into civil war. RLS was also concerned by the growing influence that imperialist powers were having on the archipelago, and he worried that the Samoans were blissfully unaware as Britain, the U.S., and Germany all vied for greater control over this supposedly independent island nation. He could see the enormous potential that Samoa offered by its strategic position and abundance of natural resources, but he also despaired at the lack of motivation amongst the majority of Samoans to do anything with them. In reference to Jesus' Parable of the Talents, RLS wrote: '*What are you doing with your talent, Samoa? Your three talents, Savaii, Upolu and Tutuila? Have you buried it in a napkin? You have rather given it out to be trodden under feet of swine … and I repeat to you that thing which is sure: if you do not occupy and use your country, others will.*' He was soon proved correct, and within six years of his writing those lines, the country had been colonised by both Germany and America to create German (later Western) Samoa and American Samoa respectively.

While much is made of the chronic illness that plagued RLS for nearly all his life, little is ever mentioned of the battles that Fanny stoically faced with her own physical and mental health. She had never particularly liked Samoa or trusted the Samoans, and initially agreed to settle on the island purely for her husband's benefit. She was just 17 years old when she married for the first time and became a mother soon after, before leaving her philandering husband and moving to Europe with their three young children, successfully supporting them all with her work as a magazine writer. Her youngest son, Hervey, contracted tuberculosis while they were in Paris and died soon after, aged just five. It was during this time that she met RLS, and she felt very conflicted by the advances of this young man while she was still legally married to her husband. She could be forgiven for her reluctance to give in to RLS's demands that she separate – there was still a considerable stigma surrounding divorce at the time – and she appears to have returned to California in order to try to salvage her marriage for one last time instead. RLS would eventually follow her across the Atlantic and persuade her otherwise, but he was hardly the model of vigour and vitality, and she spent the rest of his life as his personal nurse, constantly searching for remedies that would reduce his suffering. It is unclear what exact illness Fanny suffered from, and some biographers of RLS have even accused her of hypochondria and attention-seeking, but there is no doubt that in Samoa she experienced a period of severe mental turmoil. She suffered from hallucinations and disorientation, and RLS seems to have been only too aware of the effects that his own ill health was having on his wife. Fanny continued to write articles and short stories in Samoa, as well as becoming an enthusiastic artist, but she had to spend most of her energy on keeping RLS, Lloyd, and her mother-in-law happy. There's no doubt their marriage suffered as a result, but however bad-tempered and irritable she could be, she was a selfless and dedicated carer to her husband throughout their relationship. In 1893, RLS took a rare trip away from Samoa after an outbreak of measles on the island put him at high risk, and it was decided that he should seek refuge in Hawai'i until the situation had improved. Unfortunately, one of his servants contracted the disease and introduced it onto their ship, meaning that RLS arrived in Waikiki an extremely sick man. Fanny had stayed behind in Samoa but was immediately summoned for, and she dutifully travelled to Hawai'i and nursed him back to health yet again. It was to be the last time that RLS ever left his island home.

On 2nd December 1894, RLS and Fanny invited some American friends over to celebrate the previous week's Thanksgiving Day, and that evening Aunt Maggie wrote in her diary how content the whole family had been, with everyone having seemingly overcome their various ailments for the time being. The next day, however, all of that changed, and as RLS was helping his wife to prepare the evening meal by making homemade mayonnaise, he suddenly collapsed onto the floor. They struggled to lift him into an armchair, and eventually onto a bed, while Lloyd hurried to Apia on horseback to summon assistance. Two separate doctors came to assess him, but both agreed that he was beyond any form of medical treatment. One of those doctors, an expat who had never met RLS before, foolishly asked himself out loud: *'how could someone with arms this thin write for a living?'*, a comment for which Fanny would never forgive him or let him set foot in their house again. RLS never regained consciousness and died at 8pm on 3rd December 1894, aged just 44. After a near lifetime plagued by tuberculosis and other lung problems, it was ultimately a brain haemorrhage that had caused the author's untimely death.

RLS had made two requests regarding his funeral: firstly, that he be buried wearing the same boots in which he'd walked all over the Samoan countryside, and secondly, that his grave should be at the top of Mount Vaea. Since there was no access road to the summit at the time, a team of locals spent all of that night hacking out a path up the impenetrable mountain. People came from all over Samoa to pay their respects to the much-loved Tusitala, and the task of carrying his coffin up the steep slope became an almost Sisyphean one, with a team of men having to be tied to one another with ropes to prevent them from falling back down. RLS was buried in the exact spot he had requested, and the Samoan chiefs placed a ban on the use of firearms around the summit, so that his gravesite would always be accompanied by birdsong. This same restriction was applied more recently when the idea of building a cable car up to the top of the mountain was proposed, but since it could also have become a threat to the sound of nature over the author's grave, the project was quickly cancelled. Tusitala's grave is decorated with two metal plaques, one containing the bible verses from Ruth 1:16-17 in Samoan and adorned with a hibiscus flower and a thistle, while the other contains the text from his own poem *Requiem*.

RLS modestly referred to his four years in Samoa as *'the afterpiece of life'*, but they were in fact highly formative and productive years for the Scottish author. Beyond his local political activism, he enjoyed a diverse social life and saw himself as a Highland Chieftain watching over his extended clansmen. He led his household in evening prayers, suggesting his own belated return to Christianity, and even dressed his Polynesian servants in tartan uniforms, proving that Villa Vailima really was 'Little Edinburgh' in Samoa! Most significantly, he wrote over 700,000 words during those years, in a mix of poems, letters, fiction, and historical romance, with some of his works set in Scotland and others in the South Pacific. RLS's love for Samoa and its people has been well documented, but much less is written about the high regard in which he was held by the Samoans. As a token of their gratitude for his unwavering support, the local chiefs organised for a direct road to be built from Apia to Villa Vailima, which they insisted on naming 'The Road of the Loving Heart'. The road still stands today.

Afterword

Soon after the sudden death of her son, **Margaret Stevenson** returned to Scotland to mourn, where she died three years later. She is buried in the Stevenson's family plot at the New Calton Cemetery in Edinburgh.

Lloyd Osbourne had collaborated with RLS on three of his later books, including *The Wrecker* and *The Ebb-Tide*, and he was subsequently appointed the U.S. Vice-Consul in Samoa. He eventually became an author in his own right, although he never achieved the same degree of success as his stepfather.

Fanny Stevenson wrote of her husband's death: '*His life had been one long romance and he hoped to have a romantic end; the artist in him demanded that completeness. To grow old, he could not bear. He has had his wish and, for that, I try to be thankful, though all the rest of my life will be empty and lonely.*' She did indeed suffer from a deep depression afterwards, and she eventually decided to sell Villa Vailima and move back to California, where she slowly rebuilt her life. When she died in 1914, her ashes were returned to Samoa and buried on Mount Vaea, alongside her beloved RLS.

Villa Vailima was used by the Governor of German Samoa for his residence, and subsequently occupied by the New Zealand Government after WWI. Since 1994 it has housed the Robert Louis Stevenson Museum, a popular tourist attraction for those visiting Samoa. While the house has been decorated in keeping with the style of the late 19th century, very few of the artefacts are in fact original; however, the steep walk up to the grave of RLS is a highly worthwhile pilgrimage to make, and an excellent viewpoint from which to contemplate the life of this remarkable Scotsman alongside the words that he penned for his own tomb:

Under the wide and starry sky,
Dig the grave and let me lie.
Glad did I live, and gladly die,
And I laid me down with a will.

This be the verse you grave for me:
Here he lies where he longed to be.
Home is the sailor, home from the sea,
And the hunter home from the hill.

9. The Hermit of the South Pacific

'I chose to live in the Pacific Islands because life there moves at the sort of pace which you feel God must have had in mind originally when he made the sun to keep us warm and provided the fruits of the earth for the taking.'

– Tom Neale

While Alexander Selkirk was almost certainly the real-life inspiration for the character of Robinson Crusoe, Daniel Defoe's fictional account was apparently so believable that many people thought the story to be the biography of a real person. The tale went on to inspire countless other books and films about castaways and desert islands, even giving rise to its own literary genre known as *Robinsonade*, in which the protagonist is removed from civilisation, usually as the result of an unfortunate accident, and made to survive alone with extremely limited resources. More recently, it has become a popular format for reality TV shows, and revisits the perennial question of whether 21st century human beings are still capable of surviving by themselves in an isolated environment. And yet one softly-spoken New Zealander managed to do exactly that for over 15 years, with very few people in Polynesia ever being aware of his existence. For those who did hear about him, he was often referred to as the 'Hermit of the South Pacific', a title he disputed since he apparently did enjoy the company of others, but he just found no greater freedom on this earth than living on an uninhabited island all by himself.

Tom Neale was born in Wellington, New Zealand in 1902 and enjoyed a typical childhood that gave little suggestion as to the path his later life would take. From a young age, his only real ambition was to go to sea, and so it came as no surprise to his parents when he enlisted with the Royal New Zealand Navy at the age of 18.

Unfortunately for Neale, his role as an apprentice engineer meant that he spent most of his time below deck in the confined spaces of the engine room, and he saw very little of the ocean that he'd so dreamed of sailing. Even when they did dock at ports in the Pacific and he was allowed to disembark, he was given a very brief amount of time on shore, meaning that he could usually only visit the port area, which in the case of most Pacific Islands is never their most attractive feature. Neale discovered that a ship's visit to Samoa really only meant a few hours in the capital, Apia, and likewise all that he saw of French Polynesia was the slightly unsavoury side of Papeete. Disillusioned by this inability to really explore the South Pacific, he decided to leave the Navy after four years and spent the next six years island-hopping throughout the region. He paid for his travels by working on inter-island cargo ships for months at a time, or planting crops and clearing bush if he felt like basing himself on land instead. Either way, he managed to live on several of the islands of French Polynesia, the Cook Islands and Samoa, and quickly became enchanted by the region. After ten years away from home, he eventually returned to New Zealand, only for his father not to recognise by now which 'Tom' was calling him from the railway station and asking to be picked up!

Neale struggled to settle back into life in New Zealand, and after only a few months the lure of the South Pacific proved too strong yet again. This time he wanted to settle down on one island, and he chose the delightful island of Moorea in French Polynesia, at a time when it was still cheap, unspoiled, and sufficiently far away from the noise of Papeete. There he was able to live the simple, Polynesian lifestyle that he so craved, nourished by a daily supply of fresh fish and tropical fruit. He built a simple cabin for himself, learned the Tahitian language, and surrounded himself with books, the one 'luxury' item that he permitted himself to spend money on. One of the authors whose books he most enjoyed during this period was Robert Dean Frisbie, an American writer who had settled in the Pacific a few years earlier, and whose accounts of remote-island living would end up being the single greatest influence on Tom Neale. He might have spent the rest of his life on Moorea had it not been for a friend who owned one of the inter-island ships telling him of a storekeeper's job that was available in the Cook Islands. The new role offered more money and more stability than his current casual work in French Polynesia, even though he was perfectly content in Moorea and had little need for the additional income. When his friend informed him that he would be picking him up the next time he called in at Tahiti, Neale had little choice but to reluctantly agree to the idea.

He found his new life on Rarotonga, the main island of the Cook Islands, to be pleasant and comfortable, and he would have stayed there for many more years if fate hadn't once again intervened. One of the first people that Tom Neale met on Rarotonga was, coincidentally, Robert Dean Frisbie himself, who had recently moved to the Cook Islands for his retirement. Over several hearty meals and bottles of rum, Frisbie and Neale struck up a close friendship, and they both shared a profound passion for the islands of the South Pacific. It was during one of these jovial evenings that Frisbie began telling his new friend about his recent stay on the atoll of Suwarrow.

Suwarrow, sometimes also written as 'Suvorov' after the name of the Russian-American Company ship whose crew first discovered it in 1814, is an uninhabited coral atoll almost 600 miles north of Rarotonga. Since it is far off the regional shipping routes, Suwarrow hasn't had a permanent population since ancient Polynesian times, and yet it has been an occasional supply stop for private yachts sailing across the Pacific, including Robert Louis Stevenson in 1890. Frisbie spent a year living on the atoll with his young family in 1942 and experienced first-hand the violent cyclone that struck the same year. They only all survived after Frisbie tied each of his children to a deep-rooted tamanu tree, while every other structure on the island disappeared in the storm. His book about their year on Suwarrow, *Island of Desire*, is now a South Seas classic, and he concluded retelling his experiences to his friend with the following words: '*Tom Neale, Suwarrow is the most beautiful place on earth, and no man has really lived until he has lived there.*'

The seed had now been firmly sown in Neale's head, and when his shipowner friend later offered him a voyage to the Northern Cooks that included delivering supplies to the Allied coast-watchers on Suwarrow, it was an invitation that he couldn't refuse. Two weeks later, having briefly set eyes on the idyllic coral atoll for himself, his mind was made up: this was where he would come back to live just as soon as he could find someone to take him there.

It took him seven more years to fulfil his dream, during which time he ran the general stores on several of the Cook Islands, before he finally learned of an inter-island cargo ship that would be sailing an unusual route to the Northern Cooks and would pass close by Suwarrow. The captain agreed to make the small detour and drop Neale off, provided that he could be ready to sail in 14 days' time. Packing for a move of this scale at such short notice was no easy feat, but Tom Neale had been mentally preparing himself for this moment for much of his life, and in reality, after having lived on numerous small islands throughout the Pacific, he knew that he would only require the bare minimum of personal possessions. For his clothing he took just two pairs of trousers, two pairs of shorts, three singlets, four shirts, two pairs of sandals, and one pair of tennis shoes (for walking on the reef, as opposed to playing any tennis!). Most importantly he needed to take the correct tools, and he spent the rest of his small budget on basic construction materials.

Many of his friends on Rarotonga were worried by his plan – after all, he was already 50 years old – and donated any items to him that they thought could prove useful. Several women even asked him if he was looking for a female companion for his adventure, but having spent most of his life as a bachelor, he was well accustomed to living by himself. Much like the Polynesians on their early migrations, he took with him certain seeds and plants that he hadn't seen on his brief visit to the island seven years earlier, and others that he felt would be most beneficial for his survival. He saved the last of his money for delicacies such as tinned beef and tobacco, and also bought himself a small collection of books, knowing that he wouldn't have access to additional literature once he stepped onto Suwarrow, and he had no idea how much, if any, passing yacht traffic there would be once he was there. Last of all, he gathered up his two cats, which he was ostensibly taking to help control the island's rat population, but in reality he knew that they would be his sole source of companionship.

With his boxes packed and all stowed in the ship's hold, he was crestfallen to receive news that the voyage would have to be postponed by a month, due to a last-minute change in the shipping schedule. Utterly deflated, Neale realised that he didn't even have enough money to spend another month on Rarotonga, and ashamedly had to request a loan from the captain who had just delivered the bad news to him. One month later the ship was finally ready to set sail, and within two weeks, on 7th October 1952, Tom Neale was at last setting foot on his new island home.

Suwarrow

The ship's other passengers were surprised to see a middle-aged foreigner preparing to disembark at this uninhabited atoll, but nevertheless, they helped him unload his few supplies and took a curious look at the ruins of the coast-watchers' shack that would serve as his new home. A few of them even helped him to fix the roof of the veranda so that he would have some protection from the tropical downpours common in these parts. Only when his fellow passengers finally left to rejoin the ship did Neale feel his first pangs of solitude, as well as a deep sense of trepidation. He had spent most of his adult life dreaming of the opportunity to live by himself in paradise, and here he now was, utterly alone.

Ever the practical man, Tom Neale gave little thought to his loneliness and set to work unpacking his belongings and clearing his new home. The Allied coast-watchers had abandoned all of their posts in the Pacific at the end of WW2, and their simple accommodation on Suwarrow had since fallen into disrepair. Despite the leaking roof, he was pleased to see that the house was of a good size, and it included a small office with a desk that he would later turn into his writing room. However, he spent those first weeks on the island doing little more than cutting away all of the overgrown vegetation and making his new home habitable again after years of neglect.

During those first few months, Neale's diet consisted mainly of fresh fish, breadfruit, papaya, and coconut, all of which were found in abundance on the main islet of Anchorage. He also planted a vegetable garden close to his hut which soon provided him with greater variety, and he tamed some of the island's wild chickens and built a rustic coop in which to house them. He was thus able to supplement his diet with fresh eggs and he also discovered some nearby rock pools that were teeming with crayfish, meaning that he and his two cats were soon able to enjoy a much more nutritious and diverse diet. For now, there was very little from 'civilisation' that he missed, except for the occasional evening in the company of friends - he would later write that he never once felt lonely during those first months and was utterly content in his own solitary world.

The only unwelcome residents with whom he had to share his island were a small herd of wild boar that had been previously introduced, and which were now happily devouring his vegetable garden and anything else that he planted. Realising that his own survival depended on eradicating these intrusive beasts, he resigned himself to having to trap and kill each one individually. Having never had to do anything this gruesome in his life before, it gave him no pleasure to build a camouflaged platform within one of the palm trees and encourage the pigs to feed beneath it, at which point he could lance a sharp spear into each of their backs and hopefully kill the animals straightaway. He could only perform this macabre act on nights that offered sufficient moonlight, and it took him several weeks to lure all of the pigs to this new feeding site. After numerous nights spent perched in his arboreal hideout, he eventually managed to eradicate all of the wild boar, but was so disgusted by the barbaric process that he couldn't bring himself to eat any of the meat and buried each one instead.

Finally at peace on his island without the constant threat to his crops and fruit trees, he realised that the one thing still missing was a boat of some kind. Suwarrow is a classic coral atoll, with numerous small islets, known in all Polynesian languages as *motu*, scattered around a large central lagoon. He was currently 'marooned' on the largest of these islets, Anchorage, but knew that access to the others could provide him with additional resources and flotsam, as well as offering him some valuable new sites to explore. He'd discovered the shell of a small boat that the coast-watchers had left behind, and he spent the following months painstakingly restoring it, berating himself for not having brought caulk with him from Rarotonga with which to repair its numerous holes. Eventually, using a mixture of rope, wooden planks, and wax, he was able to waterproof the underside of the boat, and after giving it a coat of smart green paint, he finally had his own seaworthy vessel.

By this point Tom Neale had been completely alone on his island for over ten months and yet had already managed to become totally self-sufficient. He was never lonely, and gave little thought to the outside world, although he did occasionally admit to missing a companion with whom to share all of this beauty. The rowing boat had opened up a whole new world to him, and he was finally able to explore far beyond the limits of his small islet. He found a neighbouring *motu* with vastly superior topsoil to the mainly sand found on his, and over a period of several days he was able to transport 30 bags of earth back to his vegetable garden using the tiny vessel. In August 1953 he spotted a white sail approaching his island and suddenly realised he was about to receive his very first visitors. Living by himself, he'd long given up using western clothes and wore only a Polynesian-style loincloth, more out of comfort than any modesty. Upon catching sight of the yacht making its way through the pass between the coral reef, he hurried back into his hut in order to put on a pair of shorts, just in case there were ladies on board!

The *Beyond* was carrying two American couples who were sailing across the Pacific, and the British Consul in Tahiti had mentioned that an eccentric westerner was currently living on Suwarrow and had asked them to call in and make sure that he was alive. They happily obliged, and each party was as shocked as the other to find themselves sitting on the deck of the *Beyond* drinking tea (with milk!) and discussing the world's news. Several days of utter bliss followed for Neale, and a complete change to his usual daily routine of work followed by relaxing with his cats. The Americans invited him for dinner on board each evening, with rum included, and

Neale offered them freshwater baths and restocked them with as much fresh fruit and vegetables as they wanted from his garden. He thoroughly enjoyed having company, but when after three days it was time for them to continue on their journey, he felt no urge to ask them for a ride back to civilisation, nor was he concerned that he would miss them once they had gone. Ever the practical man, he simply waved them off and returned to his shack to change from his shorts back into his customary loincloth.

It must be recognised that there were two elements of extreme good fortune that characterised Tom Neale's stay on Suwarrow, and that even he was powerless against certain life-threatening situations. Firstly, the island hadn't been impacted by any extreme weather such as the cyclone endured by Robert Dean Frisbie and his family ten years earlier, and while tropical downpours were an almost daily occurrence on Suwarrow, these provided a welcome source of fresh drinking water for Neale. The second blessing was that he had maintained good health throughout, never suffering from anything worse than a mild fever or cuts to his feet from the sharp coral. Nevertheless, his luck on both fronts was about to change, dealing him a cruel reminder of his own isolation and vulnerability.

Suwarrow once had a small pier stretching out into the lagoon, but it had been mostly washed away during the cyclone of 1942, leaving nothing but its foundations at sea level. Now with his small island so tidy and pristine, Neale realised with the visit of the American couples that he had been slightly ashamed by the state of the former pier and he set himself the task of repairing it. He spent the next six months with the sole objective of dragging every single rock and stone that had been scattered by the storm back to its original position, sometimes taking a whole day just to move one large boulder. Eventually the job was completed, but it had almost cost him his health since he'd become dangerously fatigued during those months, and he realised that there was a limit to the physical exertion he was able to do on such a simple diet. He vowed never to work that strenuously again, and he celebrated the completion of the pier by giving himself the whole of the next day off! However, no sooner had he celebrated the 'grand opening' of the pier than the needle on his barometer began to drop at an alarming rate, and he realised the island was in for a bruising storm. As the wind and rain picked up, he was barely able to sleep, and spent the night praying that the roof of his shack would withstand the gale. Eventually the storm subsided, and by early the next morning he was able to step outside his home and survey the damage. Trees had been uprooted, leaves and branches were scattered everywhere, but his shack had withstood the worst of it. However, to his utter dismay, the pier had not. A powerful storm surge had poured into the lagoon and decimated all of his backbreaking work from the last six months, leaving the pier in exactly the same condition as he had first found it.

He never again attempted to rebuild the pier, but he did continue to use his small boat to visit some of Suwarrow's other islets. One and a half years into his stay, he had rowed across the lagoon in order to plant coconuts on one of them when disaster struck. He had just set foot on the *motu* and went to hurl the iron weight that served as his anchor onto the beach, when a sudden bolt of unbearable pain ran up his entire body, and he collapsed onto the sand in agony, totally paralysed. He had previously written in his journal that his ultimate fear was being rendered immobile with no way of calling for help and thus dying a slow, agonising death all alone. He found himself lying in the baking sun for several hours and assumed that he had dislocated his back in that one jarring movement, only able to turn his head very slightly without the most excruciating pain. He knew that he must get back to his hut if he was to have any chance of surviving and raised himself onto all fours to try to cover the ten yards back to the water's edge, where his boat fortunately still lay. Overcoming unimaginable discomfort, he was able to pull himself back into the rowing boat, cut the anchor rope, and somehow paddle back across the lagoon, arriving just as nightfall began to set in. He dragged himself back into his hut, collecting just two coconuts as he staggered though the kitchen, and collapsed onto his bed where he passed out.

He spent the next four days lying there, barely conscious and unable to move anything other than his head. He was over 200 miles away from the nearest human being, and he had only received one set of visitors in 18 months so far. The situation was desperate, and his only hope was that his body would somehow recover by itself and he wouldn't starve to death in the meantime. On the fifth morning, he was woken from his feverish stupor by the sound of voices, and once he was sure that they weren't a dream, he mustered all of his energy to call out. Unbeknownst to him, two American sailors had just landed on Suwarrow, and presuming the island to be completely deserted, they almost died of fright when a voice called out to them from inside the hut. The two friends nobly stayed on the island and nursed Tom Neale back to some semblance of health, to the point that he was able to stand up again after two weeks. The timing of their arrival had been nothing short of a miracle, and when the day finally came for them to leave, Neale refused their offer of a ride to Samoa but did ask them to inform the authorities on Rarotonga that he would like to be picked up. He was no longer in a fit state to be living alone on a remote island, and he needed to see a doctor urgently. Two weeks later an inter-island schooner appeared on the horizon, and Tom Neale knew that his stay on Suwarrow had come to a premature end. He left the island with a heavy heart and distinct concern about what awaited him back in civilisation, and he took only a few of his personal belongings and the two cats away with him.

Neale arrived at Rarotonga and was relieved to discover that his back spasms had been caused by nothing more than a particularly acute case of arthritis. He was told by the doctor to avoid any unnecessary physical activity, but otherwise was cleared to lead a normal life, which Neale took to mean an immediate return to Suwarrow. However, the Resident Commissioner of the Cook Islands had different ideas and forbade him from returning there on the grounds of his own safety, and without a private yacht of his own, he depended on the government authorities for a return passage.

Six frustrating years followed, in which Neale only ever dreamed of returning to his beloved island home, and the authorities continued to forbid inter-island shipping companies from taking him. The solution to his problem came in the form of a private yacht owner with an equally adventurous spirit as Neale, who agreed to take him back to his island for a small fee, meaning the authorities were now powerless to prevent him from returning. In April 1960 Tom Neale landed on Suwarrow for a second time, now much better prepared for life on a remote atoll and with a clearer idea of the dangers that it posed. He arrived back to find his house, vegetable garden, and chicken coup all completely overgrown, and once again he spent the first month clearing away everything that nature had delivered in the previous six years. The fundamental difference this time around was that in the intervening years spent on Rarotonga, he had built himself a larger and more seaworthy rowing boat, meaning he was able to sail with relative ease between the various *motu*. He even made a second, more rustic shack for himself on one of the islets on the far side of the lagoon, where he would take 'mini-vacations' to escape the hustle and bustle of Anchorage!

Neale's second stay on Suwarrow was characterised by more visitors than the first, and while he still revelled in the raw solitude that his island home offered, he also enjoyed the moments when he welcomed guests, even if he was equally relieved when they left again afterwards. On one occasion a helicopter from a passing U.S. Navy ship landed on Suwarrow, expecting to find it totally deserted. Once he'd recovered from the ear-splitting noise after months of total silence, Neale was only too happy to trade as much fruit as the pilots could take for all the American cigarettes they were carrying, since his tobacco had run out months ago!

Tom Neale had found his personal paradise on Suwarrow and his second stay lasted for over three years, during which time he perfected the art of human survival on a remote island. His peace and solitude were nearly ruined when an American sailor together with his Samoan wife and daughter paid him a visit, only for a ferocious storm to blow their yacht onto the reef and smash it to pieces. Despite all managing to escape uninjured, it was an unthinkable tragedy for the family and potentially an equally disastrous one for Neale too, as his new visitors would now have to stay with him indefinitely. However, in spite of his initial misgivings, he ended up greatly enjoying having to share his island with his new companions and was extremely sad when they were eventually rescued two months later by a passing New Zealand Navy ship, whose attention they attracted using a mirror and the sun. So much for the 'Hermit of the South Pacific'!

Tom Neale's own stay on Suwarrow came to an end just two months after their departure. Ever the pragmatic man, he knew that he wasn't getting any younger, and he was well aware of the risk of a lonely, possibly drawn-out death by himself. His solitude was also invaded by a group of Cook Island pearl divers who spent periods of several weeks at a time on Suwarrow and completely changed the dynamic of the island while they were there. He had fulfilled his personal fantasy and decided to leave voluntarily while he was still able to do so.

Neale's love affair with Suwarrow should really have ended there, and once he returned to Rarotonga he went back to his previous life of managing the island's general store. However, there was now considerable interest in hearing about his unique experiences, and so he decided to write a memoir covering both of his stays. *An Island to Oneself* was published in 1966 and has since become a firm South Seas classic, much like the books of his mentor, Robert

Dean Frisbie. The allure of small islands can be a hard addiction to break, and now finding himself with the unexpected royalties from his book, Tom Neale decided to return to Suwarrow in 1967 for a third and final time. The pearl divers had moved on by then, and realising they were utterly powerless to stop this stubborn old man, the Cook Islands authorities even gave Neale the official title of 'Postmaster' of Suwarrow, from whom visiting yachts could buy stamps, even if they had to transport the onward mail themselves!

Tom Neale spent a further ten years on Suwarrow during his third stay, and although he never wrote about his subsequent experiences, he clearly succeeded in proving to himself that he was not, in fact, as old as he'd previously felt. When a passing yacht found him in 1977 suffering from severe abdominal pains, the owners persuaded him to come back to Rarotonga with them, where he was diagnosed with advanced stomach cancer. He died six months later and is buried in the cemetery next to the international airport.

There is a compelling satisfaction to reading about other people fulfilling their fantasies, and Tom Neale is undoubtably an inspiration to anybody who has ever dreamed of living by themselves on a desert island. His own legacy became slightly more complicated when it was revealed that he had left a young family behind on Rarotonga when he first went to live on Suwarrow, although his daughter recently confirmed how proud the family were of her father's achievements. Neale was never someone who sought any recognition for the lifestyle choices that he made, nor was he particularly comfortable with his newfound celebrity status amongst the yachties who would stop by and visit him. Today the island of Suwarrow remains almost as isolated and infrequently visited as it was back in Tom Neale's day, even if this particular atoll will always be inextricably linked to the spirit of one solitary New Zealander.

10. The Troubled Life of Paul Gauguin

'I am leaving in order to have peace and quiet, to be rid of the influence of civilisation. I want only to do simple, very simple art, and to be able to do that, I have to immerse myself in virgin nature, see no one but savages, live their life, with no other thought in mind but to render, the way a child would, the concepts formed in my brain; and to do this with the aid of nothing but the primitive means of art, the only means that are good and true.'

– Paul Gauguin

Paul Gauguin has become one of the most highly acclaimed and yet equally controversial artists of the 19th century, and today his works enjoy an undisputed level of global recognition and financial worth. Like many other great painters of his generation, including Claude Monet and Vincent Van Gogh, Gauguin didn't live long enough to witness the outrageous prices that his paintings would ultimately command, and instead his life was defined by long periods of poverty, ill health, and personal hardship. His name and his art remain popular tourist attractions in French Polynesia and the South Pacific, but recent exhibitions of his works elsewhere have highlighted a public who are less willing to forgive his treatment of young women and indigenous peoples, and he remains a highly polarising figure to this day.

Paul Gauguin was born in Paris in 1848, shortly before his father, a liberal journalist and committed republican, had been forced to flee France in the wake of the failed socialist uprising against Napoleon III. Clovis Gauguin decided to take his wife, Aline, and their two young children to Peru, where Aline's family had lived for many years, and from where he hoped he would be able to continue writing and supporting the French republican cause. However, the voyage began in tragic fashion when Gauguin

Sr. suffered a fatal heart attack while the ship was rounding Cape Horn, and Aline arrived in Lima as a grieving widow with two young children.

The family spent the next six years living in the bosom of upper-class Peruvian society, where Paul and his sister were diligently cared for by a troop of housemaids and servants, while their mother took great interest in the indigenous cultures of the Andes and even started a small collection of archaeological artefacts in their home. The outbreak of civil uprisings in Peru in 1854 resulted in the family losing all of their privilege and wealth almost overnight, and Aline was forced to return to France with her young children and take a job as a dressmaker in order to support them. She was ultimately unable to care for Paul and instead sent him away to stay with his paternal grandfather in the city of Orléans, where he attended a prestigious Catholic boarding school but was also bullied for his poorly spoken French (he had been raised almost entirely in Spanish up until then). One could regard his youth as being characterised by the lack of a stable father figure and an overriding sense of not fitting in – he would later describe his childhood as having been 'stateless'.

The lure of international travel and possibly the desire for camaraderie after he finished school resulted in Gauguin joining the merchant navy at the age of 17, where he served as a ship's boy on the *Luzitano*, sailing regularly between Le Havre and Rio de Janeiro. The following year he worked as a second lieutenant on the *Chili*, circumnavigating the world for 13 months and getting his first real taste of life in the tropics. In 1871 he enlisted in the French Navy, where he served as an able seaman during the Franco–Prussian War, but after six years spent almost entirely at sea, during which time his mother had died, he decided to return to Paris and take a job on dry land, initially at the *Bourse*, the French stock exchange. By the age of 23, Paul Gauguin was enjoying a successful career as a stockbroker and had also started painting in his spare time, despite the relatively late age at which to begin. His first visit to the Louvre also had a profound effect on the promising painter, and he began to study art in any free time that his stockbroking job allowed. During this period, he also married a Danish governess whom he met in Paris, Mette-Sophie Gad, and they would go on to have five children together: four sons and one daughter.

Life was progressing well for Gauguin and his young family, and most importantly of all perhaps, he felt that he was now earning a respectable income. He was beginning to move in higher artistic circles and spent time with some of the leading Impressionists of the day, despite the group still being regarded as revolutionary and unorthodox by the French establishment. Gauguin enjoyed some early success with his own painting, and in 1879 he was invited to exhibit his works alongside prominent artists such as Pissarro, Degas, and Monet. There is a noticeable influence in his early canvases from contemporary French Impressionism, and he also began collecting paintings by fellow Impressionists, a business venture that he'd learned from his mother's partner during her later years.

Unfortunately, everything changed drastically for Gauguin and his family in November 1882 when the Paris Stock Exchange crashed following the collapse of a major bank. He lost his job and his income overnight, with the art industry also shrinking significantly, meaning that artists such as Gauguin were suddenly unable to sell their own works and the value of their personal collections diminished enormously. This catastrophic financial event left him with no option but to become a full-time painter and dedicate himself entirely to his art. Mette decided that it would be best for the family if they relocated to Copenhagen, since her family all lived there and it was considerably cheaper than Paris. Gauguin reluctantly followed them a few months later, but he never adapted to life in Denmark and nor did he manage to sell any of his paintings there. His relationship with his wife and her family became progressively more strained, and at all of their insistences, he returned to Paris, initially with their son Clovis, before eventually sending him back to his mother when the child became unwell.

Gauguin was now free to enjoy all of the excesses of the bohemian lifestyle which he had been prevented from experiencing during his stockbroking days by the nature of his work and his young family. He was now showing signs of a complex mix of personalities: on the one hand he greatly missed the income and status that his bourgeois life had provided him with, while on the other he secretly resented and despised the capitalist system, believing instead that his true calling lay in a much more artistic and nonconformist environment. Thanks to his happy childhood in Peru and worldwide travels with the French Navy, he placed a high value on the foreign and the exotic, and aspired to one day live in the tropics again. For late 19th century Parisian society, he was without doubt an eccentric and unorthodox character, repeatedly referring to himself as a 'savage' and also insisting, completely falsely, that he was of Incan ancestry!

Gauguin's economic woes soon led him to a poor and lonely existence in the French capital, and he had no choice but to take a selection of badly paid temporary jobs in order to support himself. He later decided that it would make more economical sense if he swapped Paris for the artist enclave of Pont-Aven, a small village in Brittany on the Atlantic coast. Not only was he able to save some money here, but his art also flourished, and surrounded by a community of young artists he began to finally receive the recognition that he so craved, proudly writing to his wife that '*they respect me as the best painter in Pont-Aven ... and everyone wants my advice.*' Gauguin himself was still painting mainly landscapes and remained ever faithful to the Impressionist style of the time, with the human subjects in his paintings being of secondary importance. At the same time, the cartoons and children's illustrations of the English artist Randolph Caldecott were becoming increasingly fashionable in Brittany, and offered the local artists a humorous escape from the overly serious Impressionist approach. Caldecott's influence on Gauguin can first be seen in his depictions of the Breton people of Brittany, with much more focus now on the characters themselves, and exaggerating their features to the point of caricature.

Buoyed by his success in the French countryside, Gauguin decided to seek out the simplicity of the tropics and, in his own words '*to live like a native*'. He enjoyed depicting himself as an exotic outsider, but life in Brittany was never going to be interesting enough for him, and he decided that it was time for him to leave Europe for good. He initially went to Panama, where the construction of the Canal offered the opportunity of additional work, but failing to find any success with his art there, he moved to the island of Martinique, a French colony in the middle of the Caribbean. The intensity of the sun in the tropics was something he could never have experienced in Brittany, and Gauguin was intoxicated by the array of bright colours that greeted him. '*Colour! What a deep and mysterious language, the language of dreams*', he wrote from Martinique, as he began to employ an exaggerated colour palette as a way of portraying the emotion-fuelled world that he was experiencing.

Back in Europe, the art dealer Theo Van Gogh made his most expensive acquisition to date when he bought Gauguin's *The Mango Trees, Martinique* for 400 francs, before his older brother Vincent traded two of his own paintings for *On the Banks of the River at Martinique*, also by Gauguin. It was exactly the kind of validation that Gauguin so desperately sought from his peers and a defining moment in his development as an artist. It fully justified his decision to have left Europe for the tropics, and he felt he was no longer being seen as a marginal Impressionist, but rather as the leader of a new, post-Impressionist movement.

Gauguin contracted malaria in Martinique, and despite being sick and penniless, he was able to return to France for free thanks to a government scheme that guaranteed the repatriation of any

French national who became bankrupt on colonial soil. Describing his experience in the Caribbean, he wrote: '*It was only there that I felt like my real self, and one must look for me in the works I brought back from there rather than those from Brittany, if one wants to know who I am.*' However, it was actually to Brittany that he returned, and back to the Pont-Aven school, where he and several other artists continued experimenting with the bold use of colour and, influenced in particular by Japanese art, the employment of rich, mystic symbolism in their paintings. In the meantime, Theo and Vincent Van Gogh had long been dreaming of establishing an artists' community in the peaceful city of Arles, in the south of France, and considered the 40-year-old Gauguin to be the perfect artist to lead it. Artist communes were very popular in Japan at the time and seen as a way for painters to learn from and inspire each other, ultimately benefitting everyone's art. Vincent Van Gogh saw Gauguin as a genius and his future mentor, and his brother Theo persuaded the reluctant Gauguin to relocate to Arles by offering him a monthly salary of 150 francs, money which Gauguin planned to use to travel back to Martinique.

So began one of the most explosive and short-lived associations between two renowned artists, and despite their time together starting amicably enough, when Gauguin announced that he didn't much care for Arles and was only there to finance his inevitable return to the Caribbean, Vincent quickly became paranoid about his hero abandoning him. During their two months together, Van Gogh produced some of his most famous masterpieces, including *Still Life: Vase with 15 Sunflowers* and *Starry Night Over the Rhone*. However, a competitive undercurrent between the two artists also emerged, one that saw each man paint his own version of the same scene, such as Gauguin's *Night Café at Arles*, which was his rendition of Van Gogh's *The Night Café*. It was a living arrangement and an artistic relationship that many experts consider to have been doomed from the start, due to them both having their own eccentricities and differing painting styles. Gauguin was slow and methodical, while Van Gogh was capable of finishing paintings within only a few hours. Gauguin found Van Gogh to be untidy and disorganised, while Van Gogh found his idol to be distant and motivated only by money.

The dream of creating an artists' colony in Arles lasted for just 63 days, and Gauguin was finding the Dutchman's hallucinations and erratic behaviour increasingly alarming. While the exact details of their final interaction remain unclear, the tempestuous relationship between the two came to a dramatic climax two days before Christmas in 1888. Sitting in a bar together, Van Gogh supposedly began the altercation by throwing a glass of absinthe at Gauguin's head, at which point Gauguin reacted by declaring that he would be returning to Paris the following day for good. This announcement of Gauguin's imminent departure was seemingly too much for Vincent's fragile state of mind, and he confronted Gauguin in the street with an open razor, before inexplicably cutting off the lower part of his own left ear. By the time the bandaged Van Gogh was discovered the next morning, Gauguin was well on his way back to Paris, and the two artists would never again meet in person; they did, however, maintain contact with each other by letter, right up until Van Gogh's suicide in a French mental asylum in 1890, at the age of just 37.

Gauguin arrived in Paris utterly penniless, but soon decided that his next artistic destination would be the Polynesian island of Tahiti, where his 'primitive' style would be much better suited and he could finally be free of the bourgeois, materialistic society that surrounded him in Europe. An auction of his works was organised in Paris, and to the great benefit of his finances and his own self-esteem, 29 of his paintings were sold. He paid one last visit to Mette and his five children in Copenhagen and, having assured them that he would return a rich man, he set sail for the South Pacific on 1st April 1891.

He disembarked in Papeete, the capital of Tahiti, with the fantasy that he was Adam returning home to the Garden of Eden, but he was immediately disappointed by the extent to which the city had been westernised by its colonial leaders. He chose to move to the opposite, less-developed side of the island and to live in a simple bamboo hut which brought him into much closer contact with the local Tahitians. Captivated by the beautiful scenery and the exotic islanders, he enjoyed a period of high artistic output and innovation in Tahiti, producing over 60 paintings and wooden sculptures during the course of his 18-month stay. He regularly borrowed influences from the local folklore and incorporated them into his own works, clearly visible in his most famous painting from this period, *la orana Maria* ('Ave Maria'), in which he transforms the Christian figures of the Virgin Mary and baby Jesus into a Tahitian mother and child.

There is an undeniable eroticism in this and many of his other paintings of Polynesian women, and he was developing a rich and bold style that was completely unknown to his audiences in 19th century Europe. Gauguin also wrote a highly fanciful memoir about his stay on Tahiti, *Noa Noa* ('scented land'), but it was widely criticised for portraying Tahiti in an overly-romanticised manner, and Gauguin appears to have borrowed greatly from the experiences of others. It's much more difficult to know how he really felt about Tahiti, although his numerous paintings from that period all display an irresistible vibrancy of colours, highlighting the beauty of both the island and its inhabitants.

As had been the case during most of his artistic career up until that point, Gauguin was once again struggling financially. His agent in France had only managed to sell two of his Tahitian pieces, and his earlier paintings were now being contrasted unfavourably with those of his rival Van Gogh. Added to this, his health had begun to worsen: he had contracted syphilis before he left France, and was now also suffering from heart arrhythmia, weight loss, and a host of tropical diseases. He had taken a 13-year-old Tahitian 'wife' while he was there, with whom he had even fathered a child, but nevertheless he was lonely, unwell, and destitute. Again, the French government came to his rescue by covering the cost of his passage home, and his poetic parting words to Tahiti convey an unexpectedly positive outlook on the whole experience: '*Farewell, you exquisite, hospitable, land of beauty and freedom! Indeed, these ignorant savages have taught the old civilised crew a thing or two: many an insight, and the art of being happy. I leave two years older but twenty years younger.*'

There is no doubt that Gauguin held the Tahitian people in high regard, although he also felt that they were being exploited by the French colonial authorities and that their cultural identity was being gradually eroded by western influences. Much of the artwork he produced during this period would go on to be his most prized, although it was given little recognition at the time. He returned to France in 1893, where he played on his exotic reputation by regularly dressing in Polynesian garb and producing paintings with Tahitian subjects, and he also took a new foreign lover, this time a Javanese girl named Anna. He received a sizeable inheritance of 15,000 francs from his uncle Isidore soon after his return, money that he spent on himself and the continuation of his frivolous lifestyle, and he completely failed to take his long-suffering wife Mette into account, who was still devotedly raising their five children back in Denmark.

An exhibition of Gauguin's works from Tahiti was organised in Paris, consisting of 46 paintings and 2 sculptures, but the public's reception was unfavourable, and his style was criticised for being too childish and crude. Not to be deterred by yet more negative reviews, he insisted on sticking with his South Seas subject matter, and he even attempted to rekindle his art school in Brittany, although by this time everyone had long since moved on. In Concarneau, not far from Pont-Aven, Gauguin got into a drunken fight with a group of local sailors and ended up with a broken ankle, an injury from which he never fully recovered, and it caused him considerable discomfort for the rest of his life. Anna left him while he was convalescing in hospital, even going so far as to ransack his flat in Paris before she vanished. To add insult to injury, the brawl in Concarneau resulted in legal proceedings against him, leading to even more financial hardship and the disappearance of any remaining faith in the French judicial system. Gauguin made up his mind to leave Europe for good (again) and hastily arranged yet another auction of his works in order to raise funds for his travels, although this time not a single one of his paintings sold. He even suffered the ignominy of having to buy some of his works himself in order to meet the minimum price set by the auction house. Feeling despondent and let down by his so-called supporters, Gauguin set sail to French Polynesia for the second time, hopeful of rediscovering a society which he felt had maintained much of its purity and innocence.

It was a relief for Gauguin to be back in the tropics, and he appreciated the warm welcome that he received in Tahiti from both friends and dignitaries, although he was disappointed to see some of the recent technological advances such as the introduction of electricity. As with his first visit, he began by staying in Papeete but soon tired of city life and the increased colonial presence, and later moved to a simple cabin in the interior of the island. His former Tahitian 'wife' had settled down with someone else in the meantime, and so he took another young partner, this time a 14-year-old girl called Pau'ura. Incredible as it sounds, Tahitian mothers actually sought Gauguin out as a partner for their young daughters, and the fact that these relationships were all conducted openly and in the public eye, only confirms that this was an accepted practice in the South Pacific at that time.

Judging from his correspondence with friends back in France, this first year back in Tahiti was one of the happiest periods in Gauguin's life, however somewhat predictably, this state of contentment didn't last for long, and he was soon being plagued by financial problems and ill health once again. He was still sending a regular supply of canvases back to Europe to be sold, albeit with limited success, and meanwhile he was having to take arsenic to reduce the pain of the blisters and infection from his gammy ankle. When the French Ministry of Arts agreed to pay Gauguin a grant of 200 francs in order to help him, he was so offended by this paltry sum of money that he sent it back to them. His mental health was deteriorating at an even quicker rate than his physical wellbeing, and he was being tormented by persistent bouts of melancholy and suicidal thoughts. Further tragic news arrived from Europe in the form of a letter from Mette announcing that their only daughter, Aline, had died of pneumonia, thus plunging Gauguin into an even deeper state of depression. It was then that he made up his mind: if his situation hadn't improved by the end of that year, he would take his own life.

In one final outpouring of artistic expression, he decided to paint his most thorough study of the human condition, now beyond caring about how it was received by art critics or any potential buyers. He felt that he had nothing to lose at this point, and without doing any preparatory sketches or plans, he simply painted straight from his palette onto the largest canvas that he'd ever produced: *'I have put all my energy into it one more time before I die, so painful a passion in such dreadful circumstances, so clear and accurate a vision, that there is no trace of precociousness, and life blossoms forth from it.'* The result was one of his most astonishing and profound paintings, focusing on the complete human life cycle and man's predicament from birth until death. *Where Do We Come From? What Are We? Where Are We Going?* is now on display at the Museum of Fine Arts in Boston and is considered to be one of Gauguin's greatest masterpieces.

Soon after completing his monumental work, it is said that Gauguin retired to the hills and consumed a large measure of arsenic, with the intention of ending his life. However, such was the quantity of poison that he ingested, he apparently vomited the entire dose back up and therefore failed dramatically in this venture too. He had to take himself to the local hospital and announce apologetically what he had just done, although amazingly he suffered no long-term consequences from his close taste of death. While he was recuperating, his loyal agent in Paris managed to make a quick sale of *Where Do We Come From? What Are We? Where Are We Going?* and Gauguin's financial worries were alleviated, even if only temporarily. Furthermore, a collector in France finally agreed to offer him a respectable annual salary of 3,600 francs plus materials, and guaranteed to purchase every single painting that he sent back to Europe for a modest price. Even if Gauguin considered this to be a paltry sum of money compared to what artists in his homeland were earning, it was at least enough for him to live comfortably in Tahiti.

By 1901, Gauguin had grown tired of life on the main island of French Polynesia, and the Tahitian women had presumably also lost interest in this gaunt and ageing man riddled with leg sores. Ever since he'd been shown some intricate carvings from the Marquesas Islands during his first stay in Papeete, he had dreamed of living on one of the 12 volcanic islands situated almost 1,000 miles northeast of Tahiti. The Marquesas are some of the most remote islands in the world, and even today remain proudly independent in spirit, despite having been a French protectorate since 1842. Gauguin believed he would be less exposed to the advances of technology in this isolated archipelago and be able to return to a more authentic and 'savage' way of life. He chose to settle on the island of Hiva Oa, at that time the administrative centre of the group, where he purchased a parcel of land from the Catholic Church and built himself a traditional bamboo cabin, which he christened 'The House of Pleasure'. His home became a popular gathering place for the locals, often involving debauched parties and the consumption of alcohol, all of which made Gauguin deeply unpopular with his Christian neighbours. By now, he was beset by the combined effects of an irregular heartbeat, leg ulcers, syphilis, and was possibly also addicted to the morphine which he was taking to numb the pain of all three. He contemplated moving to Spain for treatment but was persuaded by his agent (and sponsor) in France that leaving the Pacific would destroy the myth of Gauguin the South Seas painter.

By moving to the Marquesas, Gauguin had evaded several ongoing court cases against him in Tahiti, but justice finally caught up with him on Hiva Oa, this time for not paying his taxes. He was sentenced to three months in prison and ordered to pay a fine of 500 francs, a sum which, unsurprisingly, he didn't have. Ultimately, he never paid the fine nor did he serve a single day of his prison sentence, as two heart attacks suffered in quick succession resulted in his instant death on 8th May 1903. He was 54 years old, and unsurprisingly given the trajectory of his life up until that point, he died alone and penniless.

Paul Gauguin was buried in the Calvary Cemetery on Hiva Oa, in the only grave not to be adorned with a Christian cross but rather with a bronze cast of one of his sculptures, as he had specifically requested. There was an outpouring of grief from the locals when news of his death spread around the island, since he had been a popular, if eccentric, member of their community for the previous two years. It took much longer for the news to reach Europe, where a hurried auction of Gauguin's last paintings in Tahiti managed to raise 4,000 francs, which was sent to his long-forgotten wife, Mette.

Legacy

Only a few days before Gauguin died, a letter had arrived from his agent in France informing him of the successful sale of his most recent paintings, and that '*these days you are referred to as that exceptional, magnificent artist who sends in his bewildering but inimitable works from the middle of the Pacific Ocean.*' While this may have been a slight exaggeration in order to keep him painting, it was the final irony in a life full of failures and new beginnings that Gauguin should receive the recognition he so craved from his European audiences just days before his death. Many years would pass before his art began to receive the worldwide notoriety that it currently enjoys, although his unique style had influenced an entire generation of artists such as Pablo Picasso and Henri Matisse long before then. In the last 40 years the prices of his art have reached stratospheric levels, with his painting *Te Fare* ('The

House') having now been auctioned three times: first in 1895 for the equivalent of $90, then in 1991 for $9.7 million, and finally in 2017 for $25.2 million. Similarly, *Nafea faa Ipoipo* ('When Will You Marry?') was sold for an eye-watering $210 million in 2015, making it the fourth most expensive painting ever.

Art historians today regard Paul Gauguin as one of the pioneers of the post-Impressionist movement in Europe, a rebellious *bon vivant* who escaped the shackles of bourgeois society to create a unique style all of his own. Others see him as nothing more than a charlatan who labelled himself a noble savage in order to satisfy his perverted South Sea fantasies and improve the sales of his art back home. His human legacy was to leave behind numerous children who never knew their father, several of them born to pubescent Tahitian girls who were also the subjects of his paintings, all of which has made recent exhibitions of his work even more complex. International museums are today forced to consider carefully their presentation of Gauguin, and in certain parts of the world it would appear to be only a matter of time before he is either sidelined or cancelled completely. Attitudes towards Gauguin are noticeably more tolerant in the South Pacific, where his art is still celebrated and widely reproduced, and is often seen as a reminder of much more innocent times. Judging Gauguin's own behaviour by current moral standards is a dangerous and futile exercise, and only time will tell how modern society continues to view this mercurial French virtuoso. Whatever the public ultimately decides, it is unlikely that there will be another artist quite like Paul Gauguin ever again.

11. Inspiring Moby Dick: The whaleship *Essex*

'Call me Ishmael. Some years ago - never mind how long precisely - having little or no money in my purse, and nothing particular to interest me on shore, I thought I would sail about a little and see the watery part of the world.'

– Herman Melville (Moby Dick)

When Herman Melville penned one of the most famous opening lines to any novel in American literature, he had never visited the whaling capital of Nantucket and had abandoned the only whaling ship he'd ever worked on at its first port of call in the Marquesas Islands. Jumping ship at Nuku Hiva led to his writing two South Sea classics, *Typee* and *Omoo*, and would set Melville on a path first as a travel writer and subsequently as a novelist, culminating in the creation of one of the great American works of literature, *Moby Dick*.

While serving as a deckhand on his first and only whaleship, Melville read an account about a rare albino sperm whale, christened Mocha Dick by whalers after being sighted for the first time near the island of Mocha in southern Chile, and which was notorious for being particularly difficult to hunt. Having spent those months in the close company of whalers, Melville must have also heard about the gruesome events that took place on the whaleship *Essex* 20 years earlier, as numerous versions of the story had already found their way into whalers' folklore by then. When Melville happened to meet a young man by the name of William Henry Chase on another whaling ship in the South Pacific and realised that he was the teenage son of Owen Chase, First Mate on the *Essex*, he was excited to speak with the boy and to read a copy of his father's first-hand account. Melville was both shocked and moved by what he read, particularly since he was sailing in the same waters as the events described in those pages, later admitting that '*the reading of this wondrous story upon the landless sea, and close to the very latitude of the shipwreck had a surprising effect upon me.*'

In 1850, Melville purchased a farm for himself in Pittsfield, Massachusetts, and in the same year began writing his novel about a ship captain's obsessive hunt for revenge against an aggressive white whale that had bitten off his leg. *Moby-Dick* was published the following year, although the hyphen featured only in the title, and it was dropped altogether in subsequent reprints. The book drew from a number of influences, including Melville's own experiences as a sailor and his knowledge of the mythical white whale, Mocha Dick. However, the novel's finale was undoubtedly inspired by the true story of the *Essex*, even if *Moby Dick* gives few clues as to the exact nature of events as they unfolded on board the real-life whaling ship.

The Final Voyage of the *Essex*

The *Essex* was a whaleship based on the island of Nantucket in Massachusetts, which by the late 18th century had become the whaling capital of the world, thanks to the large number of North Atlantic right whales that converged in the nearby waters. The *Essex* had already enjoyed a successful 20-year hunting career and was generally considered to be a 'lucky' ship by the crew who sailed on her. On 12th August 1819, she left Nantucket for yet another extensive voyage to the whaling grounds off South America, under the command of Captain George Pollard Jr., who was just 27 years old at the time. Pollard was joined on board by First Mate Owen Chase, with whom he'd worked on previous expeditions of the *Essex*, and together they formed part of a diverse crew of 21 men, drawn from various backgrounds and ethnicities. The routine voyage was expected to last for at least two years, depending on the time it took them to fill all of their barrels with sperm oil, with the profits divided up evenly amongst the crew at the end.

This particular voyage began ominously, when only two days after leaving Nantucket, they sailed into the middle of a violent storm that ripped through the ship's upper sails and left the *Essex* listing perilously to one side. Two of the ship's five whaleboats (open rowboats used to pursue and harpoon whales) were lost and a third one badly damaged. With only two functioning whaleboats on board, they no longer had the necessary equipment for a whale hunt, and Captain Pollard decided it would be best to return immediately to Nantucket for repairs. However, Owen Chase convinced his captain to carry on instead, concerned by the effect that turning back would have on the men's spirits, and insisting that they would be able to obtain a replacement whaleboat somewhere along the route, something that they managed several weeks later while in the South Atlantic.

By the time that the *Essex* rounded Cape Horn in January 1820, they had killed just one whale in the previous four months, and the crew's morale was unsurprisingly low, with the men facing the prospect of a lengthy voyage and almost no money at the end of it. Their fortunes improved only slightly on the west coast of South America, where they managed to harpoon one whale in Chilean waters, before sailing towards the coast of Peru and successfully catching a further ten. As they continued north into Ecuador, two significant events took place: firstly, one of the crew deserted in the port of Atacames, and secondly, the *Essex* paid an infamous visit to the Galapagos Islands. Crew members deserting ships was nothing new at the time, but it did seriously affect the whaling operation in this instance, since each whaleboat needed six men to crew it, and the additional three crewmembers were the bare minimum required to manage the *Essex* while all of the whaleboats were out hunting. The once abundant waters off Peru and Ecuador contained many fewer whales than they were expecting to find, and it appears that the effects of overfishing in the region were already starting to be felt.

While speaking with other whalers in northern Ecuador, the crew learned of a rich new hunting ground towards the southwest, in a remote part of the South Pacific known simply as the 'offshore ground'. It was much further from the coastline than whalers were ever used to venturing, however the lure of unexploited whaling grounds was too good to ignore, and they called in at the Galapagos Islands on their way to the South Pacific in order to restock their supplies. They managed to collect 360 giant tortoises which would be kept alive on board and gradually eaten over the coming months, but while on the island of Floreana, one of the crew members started a fire as a practical joke, and unaware that it was the height of the dry season at the time, the inferno rapidly spread and soon enveloped the whole island. Not only did he nearly trap several of his colleagues within the fire, but the visit of the *Essex* is also blamed for having caused the near extinction of several of the island's endemic species, including the Floreana tortoise and the Floreana mockingbird.

The crew sailed almost 2,000 miles away from the coast of South America and found themselves in totally uncharted waters for a group of whalers from Nantucket, and in a region of the South Pacific almost completely devoid of any other ship traffic or human life. Their first few days of hunting in those waters were frustrating ones, as the only whale they spotted and pursued ended up damaging a whaleboat with a swipe of its powerful tail. On 20th November, a large group of whales was eventually spotted, and the two remaining whaleboats were launched to close in on them, while Owen Chase remained on the *Essex* and continued with the repairs to the third. His colleagues successfully harpooned one of the whales, and they were in the process of having their whaleboat towed around the ocean by the angry creature while they waited for it to tire, a procedure known amongst whalers as a 'Nantucket sleighride'. While this was taking place, Chase spotted an unusually large sperm whale lying in the water on the port (left) side of the *Essex* and estimated it to be about 85 feet long, over 25% larger than the average male sperm whale. It was strange behaviour for the whale to be this close to a whaleship, but his surprise quickly turned to horror when the whale lowered its head down into the water and began charging aggressively towards them, before ramming the *Essex* at midships on the port side. The powerful collision threw the three men across the deck, and as they struggled to their feet while trying to understand what had just happened, they noticed that the whale was also momentarily dazed by the impact and had reappeared on the surface alongside the ship. Chase's hunting instincts quickly kicked in, and seeing the enormous creature at such close quarters, he hurriedly prepared a harpoon in order to try to hook the whale. However, he also noticed that the whale's tail was lying directly beside the ship's rudder and fearing that with one powerful flick it could leave the *Essex* without the ability to steer, he paused. Meanwhile, the whale, now fully recovered, swam off once more, only to turn around several hundred yards away and swim back towards the ship, this time with twice the speed and aggression. '*Here he is – he is making for us again*', one of the crew cried out, as the whale slammed into the *Essex* for a second time, on this occasion smashing a gaping hole close to the ship's bow and causing seawater to pour in. The whale then dove back down into the depths, never to reappear.

In the space of less than five minutes, Owen Chase had gone from spotting the large whale for the first time to now realising that the *Essex* was doomed, and that at any moment she would be consumed by the ocean. Only the large quantity of whale oil on board was keeping the sinking ship afloat, but Chase immediately recognised that they must salvage anything of value before their ship disappeared forever. This was the first case of a seemingly unprovoked attack in the history of whaling, and a unique situation in which the hunters suddenly became the hunted. Experts have since speculated that the whale may have confused the hammering sound from the repairs to the boat with the clicking sounds of a competing male moving into his territory, resulting in the aggressive attack. Equally possible, the protective whale may have been reacting to the hunt that was taking place in the nearby waters, and from what we now understand about the intelligence of these magnificent creatures, the whale may well have perceived the close connection between the whaleboats and the *Essex*.

Captain Pollard and the other whalers were too far away from the *Essex* to have witnessed the events as they unfolded, but once their 'sleighride' came to an end, they were astonished to see that their previously upright ship was now leaning heavily to one side and gradually slipping beneath the waves. Both whaleboats hurried back to the ship as fast as they could, only to find Chase and the other two crewmen desperately trying to salvage all of the ship's charts and navigational instruments, and as much freshwater and dry food as possible. Utterly dumbfounded, the captain asked, '*My God, Mr. Chase, what is the matter?*', to which his First Mate replied, '*We have been stove by a whale*'.

Realising that any hope of saving the ship was by now impossible, the 20-man crew divided themselves into the three whaleboats, each commanded by one of the ship's officers: Pollard, Chase, and Second Mate Matthew Joy. They crammed themselves into the three small boats that were never intended to sail long distances, having been designed with low sides especially for harpooning whales, and they were therefore completely impractical for crossing oceans. The nearest piece of land to them was over 1,000 miles away, meaning that they were also desperately short of provisions, having managed to rescue little more than a few giant tortoises, some hardtack (dry biscuits), and several barrels of freshwater. Since there were only two sets of maps and navigational equipment, Matthew Joy's boat had no option but to try to keep the other two whaleboats within sight at all times.

The crew found themselves about as far away from dry land as it was possible to be on the planet. Pollard calculated that the nearest islands to them were the Marquesas, but there was a widespread rumour amongst whalers at the time that many of the islands in the South Pacific were off limits due to being inhabited by cannibals. Pollard decided instead to sail southwest towards Tahiti, which would have been a sensible choice given that English missionaries had been there for over 20 years, but for the second time on this voyage Owen Chase persuaded him to change his mind. The First Mate believed that if they sailed due south, they would soon pick up the westerly currents that would push them towards South America, and that they couldn't avoid reaching land somewhere along the Chilean coast. Chase felt that despite the longer distance, the route offered an easier final target to aim for and a greater chance of being discovered by another ship along the way. The crew estimated that the voyage would take them a minimum of two months to complete, and they strictly rationed their provisions accordingly.

The journey south was perilous and beset by difficulties, from fierce storms that nearly sunk them, to extreme sunstroke and constant exposure to the elements. After only a few weeks at sea, the sailors had already resorted to drinking their own urine due to the lack of available freshwater, and with most of their food having been soaked by seawater, everything they ate only exacerbated their thirst. On 20th December, exactly one month since the attack by the whale and with various members of the crew at the point of death, they sighted land for the first time since their ordeal had begun and landed at the uninhabited island of Henderson, one of the four Pitcairn Islands. Amazingly, they had covered 1,500 miles by open boat without losing a single man, but there was also a cruel irony to their arrival at Henderson: if they had only reached the island of Pitcairn instead, just 93 nautical miles to the east, then their ordeal would most probably have ended there and then, since the descendants of the mutineers of HMS *Bounty* were still living in their small community on the island, having been discovered by the outside world just a few years earlier.

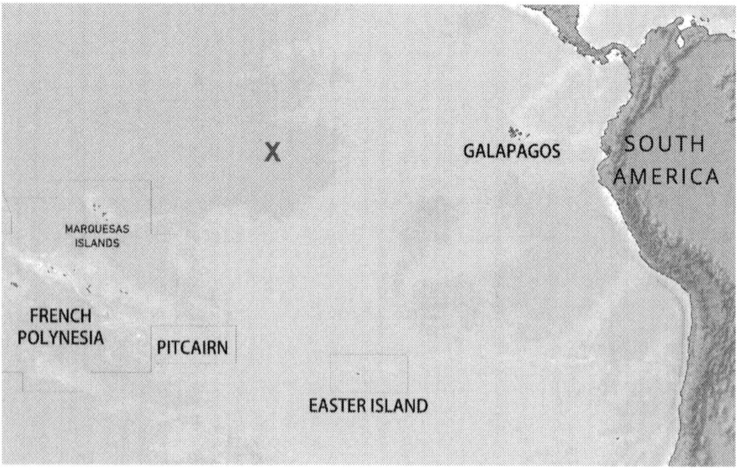

The men were thrilled to discover a freshwater spring on Henderson that was accessible at low tide, as well as crabs, seabirds, and birds' eggs on which to gorge themselves; there was also the sheer relief of no longer being cooped up with each other in leaking rowboats on tempestuous seas. Having been there for a week, they had exhausted nearly all of the island's food resources, and Pollard decided that it was time to begin their journey eastwards. Difficult as it was to leave the safety of dry land, the crew understood that their chances of being discovered on Henderson were close to zero, and that their only hope of salvation depended on alerting others of their plight. No one in the world was even aware that the *Essex* was missing, let alone that it had been rammed by a whale and sunk.

Three of the crewmembers decided that they couldn't face returning to sea, preferring instead to take their chances staying on Henderson Island in the hope that they would eventually be rescued. Unsurprisingly, their decision was met with relief by the rest of the crew, since it meant fewer mouths to feed and slightly more space on each whaleboat. During their brief stay on dry land, Pollard had calculated they were now over 3,000 miles away from the South American coast and accepted that they no longer had the provisions nor the energy for such an arduous journey. He decided to make for Easter Island instead, which although none of them had ever visited, was less than 1,000 miles away - it appears they were now willing to overlook their prejudices regarding South Pacific islanders and their dietary choices!

On 27th December 1820 the party of now 17 men set sail from Henderson, and within two weeks Second Mate Matthew Joy became the first member of the group to succumb to their ordeal. He had been suffering from an unknown illness, probably tuberculosis, from well before the encounter with the whale, and his already weakened body was unable to endure the extreme conditions and poor diet. He was given a traditional sea burial, and command of his boat passed on to Obed Hendrix, who soon realised that Joy had been mismanaging their rations and that provisions on their whaleboat had almost run out. During a violent gale the following day, Chase's boat became separated from the other two, and they spent the next week alone at sea, desperately praying that they would be reunited with their companions. Chase's boat had only five occupants on board since Henderson, and that soon became four when Richard Peterson died and was also buried at sea, as was the maritime custom. Three weeks later another crewmember on Chase's boat died, only this time they didn't immediately bury him, but rather stowed his body on board. Something had changed in the minds of the men, and just one day before consuming their final rations of hardtack, they were forced to confront one of the greatest taboos of the human condition: cannibalism.

Little did the men in Chase's boat know, but those in Hendrix's vessel had also exhausted their own food supplies by 14th January, and despite Pollard generously agreeing to share his provisions with the other crew, within a week both boats had completely run out of food. Over the course of the following seven days, four more men died from starvation, three from Hendrix's boat and one from Pollard's, and each time it was agreed that they had no choice but to keep the corpses on board. Completely independently of each other, the crew of the two sailing groups had arrived at the same grim conclusion, namely that if they were going to survive themselves, then they would need to consume the flesh of some of their former shipmates. Ironically, if the recently stranded crew of the *Essex* had made directly for either the Marquesas or Tahiti and run the risk of meeting cannibals (highly unlikely by 1820), they would have been spared the fate of having to resort to this same practice themselves. Despite their dire circumstances, the men were still tormented by the gruesome act that they were committing: '*Humanity must shudder at the dreadful recital*' Owen Chase would later write about their behaviour, and they endeavoured to perform the deed in the most dignified way possible. Given that there was so little flesh left on each corpse, the sailors generally removed the edible organs and cooked them over hot stones, before sewing the body back up and committing it to the sea.

On 28th January, Obed Hendrix and his companions became separated from Pollard's boat in a ferocious storm and would never see either their captain or any other crewmember from the *Essex* ever again. From the original six men who had left Henderson Island, Hendrix's boat now contained just three, and they were going to have to navigate their way to safety without any maps or visual cues. Four men remained alive on Pollard's boat, but they were in no physical state to begin any kind of search for Hendrix and his party. By 1st February they had once again run out of food, although this time there were no recently deceased corpses with which to sustain themselves, and the grim decision was taken that one of the four men would have to voluntarily sacrifice himself for the survival of the others. Lots were drawn amongst the sailors and Pollard's 18-year-old first cousin, Owen Coffin, drew the black spot, at which point the captain immediately offered to take the young man's place; after all, he had promised the boy's mother that he would take good care of him for the duration of the voyage. Coffin is said to have replied: '*No, I like my lot as well as any other*', and straws were again drawn, this time to decide who would be the unfortunate person tasked with killing him. His good friend Charles Ramsdell drew the short straw and was handed Pollard's revolver for the unenviable task. Thanks to Owen Coffin's sacrifice they managed to keep themselves alive for a further ten days before the other sailor perished and was also cannibalised. By the end, just Pollard and Ramsdell remained in their whaleboat.

Meanwhile on Owen Chase's boat, the three surviving men were so weak by now that they were incapable of doing anything beyond simply lying on the floor, unable to steer or sail, and completely resigned to their fate. They had run out of food on 15th February and seemingly never considered the same extreme act of sacrifice that had taken place on Pollard's boat. Suddenly, on 18th February, and just days from certain death, they spotted the white sails of a large ship in the distance and put every last ounce of their energy into chasing her down. The British ship

Indian eventually spotted the whaleboat and rescued the three dying sailors from their horrendous ordeal. Their mouths were so dry that they were unable to speak, and when asked who they were, Chase could only utter three words: '*Essex … whaleship … Nantucket.*' Eighty-nine tortuous days after the sinking of the *Essex*, they had been plucked from the ocean near to the coast of Chile and were described by the captain who rescued them as having been '*the picture of suffering and misery*'. The three survivors were taken to the port of Valparaiso, where they were transferred onto a U.S. Navy frigate, USS *Constellation*, and whose doctor was able to oversee their gradual recovery.

Four days after Chase and his party were rescued, the whaleship *Dauphin* spotted a small boat drifting in the sea, also just off the Chilean coast. Its two inhabitants were so detached from reality by this point that they didn't even notice the *Dauphin* pull up alongside them, and then cowered in fear at the sight of other human beings. Pollard and Ramsdell had been at sea for 93 days since the sinking, and they were so embarrassed by the gnawed human bones scattered around the bottom of their boat that they desperately tried to hide the evidence in their pockets. The *Dauphin* took them aboard and later transferred them to a ship that was headed for Valparaiso, so that on 17th March 1821, the 5 survivors from the original 17 that had left Henderson Island were finally reunited with each other.

While they had been on Henderson, the crew of the *Essex* had never really known which island they were actually on, believing erroneously that it was Ducie, another island in the Pitcairn Group. As soon as Chase and his colleagues had been rescued, they informed the authorities that there were three more survivors from the *Essex* stranded on the island of Ducie, and an Australian cargo ship, the *Surry*, was told to call in at the island and look for them. The *Surry* arrived at Ducie but found no one there, and guessing correctly that there must have been a mix-up between the names of these remote islands, they called in at neighbouring Henderson just in case. There, on 9th April 1821, they found the three remaining survivors, each one just barely alive. The men had spent nearly four months alone on this uninhabited island, depending on rain showers for their drinking water and the occasional bird or sea turtle that they were able to catch for nourishment.

Aftermath

The eight survivors all eventually returned to Nantucket and were welcomed home without any criticism or judgement. Cannibalism was regarded as 'a custom of the sea', although in previous situations, the crew had only ever gone as far as using human flesh for bait with which to catch fish. However, it was reasoned that this wouldn't have been possible for the crew of the *Essex*, given the lack of marine life near the surface in that particular part of the Pacific. Even more surprisingly, all eight of the survivors returned to work on whaling ships soon afterwards, and Owen Chase also published *Narrative of the Most Extraordinary and Distressing Shipwreck of the Whale-ship Essex*, which was the same manuscript that his son, William, later shared with Herman Melville.

For Captain George Pollard Jr., returning to life in Nantucket was a much more difficult proposition, especially once it became known that he had consumed his 18-year-old cousin in order to save himself. Many people never forgave him for that particular act, and Owen Coffin's mother refused ever to be in his presence again. It is said that on 20th November each year, the anniversary of the sinking of the *Essex*, Pollard would lock himself in his room and observe a fast in honour of the lost crewmen. His maritime career never recovered either, and the first whaleship that he captained after the *Essex* was wrecked on a reef in Hawai'i during a violent storm. He was subsequently offered the command of a merchant ship which was also wrecked, and by that time Pollard was considered an unlucky captain and he was never given another position on board a ship. He lived out the rest of his days working as Nantucket's night watchman, ensuring the security of the port and its ships, until his death in 1870, aged 78. He had been just 27 years old when he captained the *Essex* on her fateful voyage, a remarkably young age to have been responsible for the lives of 19 other men during such a distressing ordeal. Owen Chase spent most of the rest of his working days at sea, even earning enough money to build his own whaleship, the *Charles Carrol*, which he successfully sailed for nearly 20 years. However, he was never able to overcome the traumatic memories of the *Essex*, and he suffered from ill health and nightmares for the rest of the life. He spent the final years of his life in a mental institution in Nantucket, where he died in 1869, aged 73.

The final mystery surrounding the fate of those on board the *Essex* was seemingly solved many years later, when a whaleboat containing three skeletons washed up on Ducie Island. While the remains were never officially identified, it is assumed that the corpses belonged to Obed Hendrix and his two companions, and that they had died at sea sometime after 28th January 1821, when they lost sight of George Pollard's boat.

One year after the publication of *Moby Dick*, Herman Melville finally decided to visit Nantucket for the first time; this was all the more surprising since the book's protagonist, Captain Ahab, and his ship the *Pequod*, both hailed from the small island off Cape Cod. He was at last able to see for himself the town about which he had written so atmospherically, and he spoke with numerous local dignitaries and members of the Nantucket whaling community. During his last night there, he briefly met with the harbour's night watchman, and well aware of the ordeal which he had suffered, Melville chose not to question him at length. He was greatly moved by his brief interaction with Captain George Pollard, and afterwards wrote: *'To the islanders he was a nobody, but to me, the most impressive man, tho' wholly unassuming, even humble – that I ever encountered.'*

While the story of the *Essex* is often considered to have been a major influence for Melville's novel, in fact it is only really obvious in the story's ending, when the white whale Moby Dick rams the *Pequod* and sinks it. Captain Ahab is caught in a harpoon line and hurled to his death, while all of the remaining crewmembers are sucked into the vortex created by the sinking *Pequod* and drown, with the exception of Ishmael. One detail that most readers fail to appreciate is that Ishmael survives by holding on to an empty coffin which had been prepared for one of the sick crewmembers, but ultimately never used. This small detail appears to be a clear acknowledgement of the sacrifice made by Owen Coffin from the *Essex* in keeping his colleagues alive for long enough to be finally rescued.

During Melville's lifetime, *Moby Dick* sold only 3,000 copies, and in fact marked his decline as a popular writer after the successes of *Typee* and *Omoo*. After a series of unsuccessful novels, Melville switched to writing poetry, but was ultimately forced to take a job as a customs inspector in New York City, a position that he kept for 19 years until his death in 1891, aged 72. In 1919, during the celebrations of the centenary of his birth, the public rediscovered the works of Herman Melville, and his novels began appealing to a broad spectrum of readers. *Moby Dick* went from near obscurity to becoming regarded as one of the finest novels in the English language, and is today a popular title for children and adults alike. It is perhaps fortunate that so little is known about the horrific events that inspired its writing, while for the few people who do, its popularity serves as a fitting memorial to the brave men of the *Essex* and their grisly ordeal in the South Pacific.

12. The Pacific Theatre of WW2

'As the sun disappeared below the horizon and its glare no longer reflected off a glassy sea, I thought of how beautiful the sunsets always were in the Pacific. Suddenly a thought hit me like a thunderbolt. Would I live to see the sunset tomorrow?'

– Eugene B. Sledge, U.S. Marines

In the space of just a few hours in December 1941, the Pacific Islands were transformed from a remote and geopolitically insignificant backwater to one of the major battlegrounds of the Second World War, ultimately becoming its deadliest campaign in terms of human casualties. The Pacific Theatre encompassed the widest geographical area of the entire war, and while its European counterpart remains the best-known campaign of WW2, events in the Pacific quickly made the Allies, and in particular the United States, have to radically rethink their military tactics. Forced to abandon their initial 'Europe First' strategy, the Allies were required to mobilise vast numbers of troops and weaponry in order to prevent the rapidly advancing Japanese war machine from conquering the entire region.

War in Southeast Asia had begun in 1937 with Japan's invasion of China, and since then America had been doing everything in its power to prevent the Japanese empire from expanding further, while simultaneously trying to remain neutral in the various conflicts. However, all of that changed instantly on 7th December 1941, when one transformative event led not only to America's immediate entry into the war, but also introduced global conflict to the Pacific Ocean for the first time in its history.

'A Date That Will Live in Infamy'

In 1940, President Roosevelt had ordered the U.S. Navy's Pacific Fleet to relocate from its traditional base in San Diego, California to the island of Oahu in Hawai'i, believing that a larger, more visible military presence in the Pacific would serve as an additional deterrent to the Japanese. Later that same year, America, Britain, and the Netherlands all placed embargoes on the sale of oil and aviation fuel to Japan, greatly disrupting the Japanese agenda of imperial expansion, and threatening to cripple the country's entire economy. With only 18 months' worth of its own oil stocks left, Japan desperately needed to obtain supplies from its neighbours in Southeast Asia, and in particular from the rich oilfields and refineries of the Dutch East Indies (modern-day Indonesia). America had been clear that it would not tolerate an invasion of these sovereign nations by Japan, whereas for the Japanese, solving their oil problem was fast becoming a national emergency, and direct war with the United States was now looking increasingly likely. With the greatest threat to Japan's expansion in Asia currently lying at anchor in Oahu's main naval port, the Japanese realised that their best chance of winning this now inevitable war was to employ the element of surprise against the U.S. Pacific Fleet.

On 26th November 1941, the Japanese Pearl Harbour strike force, made up of six heavy aircraft carriers carrying over 70 aircraft each, departed from its anchorage in the Kuril Islands, midway between Japan and Russia. The task force maintained strict radio silence throughout the ten-day sea passage in order to ensure that their intentions were never exposed, and they managed to arrive undetected to a launch area within 230 miles of Oahu. Rather than sailing due east and approaching Hawai'i from the west, they had sailed almost to Alaska and taken advantage of a lightly surveilled corridor to approach Hawai'i from the north. As the sun rose on Sunday 7th December 1941, 70 American warships were still settling into their new home at Pearl Harbour on Oahu's southern coast, and despite increased Japanese radio chatter during the previous weeks, the ships of the Pacific Fleet were lying in a state of low alert. Several crucial events which would have spoiled the attack's element of surprise were missed, beginning before dawn when the minesweeper USS *Ward* spotted a Japanese midget submarine brazenly approaching the antisubmarine netting stretched across the entrance to Pearl Harbour. Despite attacking the submarine with a depth charge and subsequently sinking it, a report of the incident wasn't passed up the chain of command in a timely manner. Secondly, a U.S. Army air search radar on Oahu's north shore picked up the main body of Japanese aircraft as they approached the island at a range of about 100 miles, but the blips on the screen were assumed to be a convoy of American B-17 bombers due to arrive from California that day and were promptly ignored. Incredibly, the Japanese air fleet had managed to breach the American defences and reach Hawai'i unnoticed, and they broke radio silence for the first time to inform their superiors back on the aircraft carriers that the element of surprise had succeeded, with the now infamous words: *'Tora, Tora, Tora!'* (Tiger, Tiger, Tiger!).

Within minutes, the first wave of Japanese fighter aircraft had pounded the anchored U.S. fleet, while dive bombers simultaneously targeted American military aircraft parked at nearby airbases, thus removing the possibility of any counter-attacks. The second wave of Japanese planes soon followed, dropping bombs on American ships anchored elsewhere around the island, as well as on those in dry docks. Japanese pilots who had by now returned to the aircraft carriers urged their Admirals to order a third sortie, this time to destroy all additional military installations such as shipyards, oil storage depots, and submarine docks, without which the U.S. would have been powerless to operate during the rest of the war. However, these requests were rejected on the grounds that the Japanese still didn't know where the American aircraft carriers were at that time, and they feared full-scale retribution if they stayed in the area for any longer.

The ferocious aerial attacks were all over within two hours, and left 19 U.S. Navy ships, including 8 battleships, either sunk or badly damaged, and nearly 200 Army and Navy aircraft completely destroyed. The human cost was equally high, with 2,400 people killed outright, including many civilians, and a further 1,000 wounded. Almost half of the casualties were serving on the USS *Arizona*, as it came under heavy Japanese torpedo fire resulting in a blazing inferno on board. By contrast, the Imperial Navy lost only 29 aircraft and 5 midget submarines, at a cost of just 64 lives. On the day following the attack, President Roosevelt gave his now famous speech before a Joint Session of Congress, who immediately and unanimously approved the declaration of outright war on Japan.

Despite the enormous loss of life, much of the infrastructure around Pearl Harbour had miraculously remained intact, and the U.S. Navy was able to recover surprisingly quickly. The fact that none of its four aircraft carriers were anchored in Pearl Harbour that day had prevented the Pacific Fleet from being utterly crippled – a considerable stroke of luck given that so much of the subsequent war in the Pacific would be fought at sea. The entrance to Pearl Harbour was also never blocked, meaning that it could remain in continuous use as a sea base and the U.S. Pacific Fleet was never prevented from regrouping. While today it is generally accepted that Pearl Harbour was a resounding tactical victory for the Japanese, it was simultaneously an enormous strategic error. The surprise attack was a bitter humiliation for America, and yet it also served to unite the various branches of the U.S. military and galvanise the American public into finally accepting that their country's troops be deployed in an international war.

The Pacific Campaign

Within hours of the attack on Pearl Harbour, the Japanese also sent a squadron of aircraft from their base in the Marshall Islands to Wake Island, a small coral atoll located halfway between

Hawai'i and Japan. The strategic importance of Wake could not be overstated, since it possessed a long runway right in the middle of the Pacific, and was a key stepping stone and refuelling stop between Japan and mainland America. Wake had been placed on the aviation map by Pan Am a few years earlier, as they sought to expand their network with new routes across the Pacific and to link the U.S. and Asia by air. The Navy had authorised Pan Am to build fuel tanks and a 48-room hotel on the island, and in 1936 the inaugural flight between San Francisco and the Philippines took off. The journey required five segments and several overnight stops, and consisted of over 60 hours of total flying time, with each ticket costing the equivalent of almost $20,000 today!

Once war with Japan had begun to look increasingly likely, the U.S. Navy had upgraded the facilities on Wake Island to include a full airstrip together with army barracks and defensive guns. Twelve fighter aircraft and a garrison of 450 U.S. Marines were permanently stationed on the island - many fewer than were needed to satisfactorily defend it, but a military presence all the same. At the precise moment when the Japanese bombers were retreating from Pearl Harbour, another of their squadrons was using the cloud cover over Wake for a surprise attack on the island, and they succeeded in killing half of the Marines and destroying eight of their fighter aircraft almost immediately. Japanese air raids followed on a daily basis for the next two weeks, and it seemed to be only a matter of time before the island and its residents would be forced to surrender to the enemy.

The surviving Marines and civilians bravely defended their island against this continuing aerial onslaught, before the first group of Japanese warships reached Wake on 11th December, consisting of two light cruisers, six destroyers, and 800 battle-ready infantry soldiers. However, the U.S. Marines and the remaining local contractors weren't going to concede without a fight, and taking up their positions behind the coastal defence guns, they waited for the landing party to approach the shore before unleashing the full might of their limited arsenal upon them. Helped greatly by the aerial support of the four remaining Grumman F4 Wildcats, the Americans managed to sink two enemy destroyers and badly damage several others, forcing the Imperial Navy to retreat. It was now the turn of the Japanese to be humiliated, and they had no option but to return 12 days later with an additional 1,500 troops for a second attempt at the invasion, at which point they did succeed in capturing the island. Nevertheless, the small but significant American victory against their first assault was seen as an enormous boost to the Allies' morale, and it was also the first notable setback suffered by the Imperial Navy during the war. It instilled much-needed confidence into the American war machine after the ignominy of Pearl Harbour and offered a ray of hope that the Japanese could be defeated after all.

The Japanese coordinated their surprise attacks in the Pacific with similar assaults across Southeast Asia, and between December 1941 and March 1942 they invaded and captured Hong Kong, Singapore, Thailand, the Dutch East Indies, the Solomon Islands, Guam, and half of New Guinea. They also attacked the Philippines, an important American base at the time, and despite early advances which the Japanese assumed would lead to a swift capture, the American and Filipino troops managed to hold out for a further four months, in one of the most bloody and protracted battles of the entire war. Their resistance against the Japanese advancement made an invaluable contribution to the position of the other Allied forces, particularly in Australia where it provided them with more time to strengthen their defences, and it forced the Japanese to send additional troops to the Philippines that they would otherwise have deployed elsewhere. Nevertheless, by the summer of 1942, the entire Pacific region was becoming increasingly dominated by Japan's purposeful advance south and east. There was a brief moment of positivity for the Allies in April of that year when an audacious bombing raid on Tokyo led by Lieutenant Colonel James Doolittle managed to breach the Japanese air defences, after they had employed the unusual tactic of taking off in their B-25 bombers from an aircraft carrier close to the Japanese coastline. Although they were only able to cause limited damage with just 16 aeroplanes, it provided yet another important boost to Allied morale and also succeeded in shattering the belief held by the Japanese that their homeland was impenetrable by attacks from the air.

The Allies had been caught off guard by the speed and efficiency of the Japanese advancement, and it took them well into 1942 before they were able to regroup and organise themselves into a more united force. This increased level of organisation was first seen at the Battle of the Coral Sea, off the northern coast of Australia, where joint American and Australian forces ambushed a Japanese offensive against Port Moresby, the capital and main port of New Guinea. Unbeknownst to the enemy, Allied codebreakers were by now able to intercept and decipher many of the Japanese communications, and thus the element of surprise which had been key to their victories at Pearl Harbour and Wake Island, was now significantly reduced. Defending Port Moresby became a vital Allied objective in order to prevent Japan from isolating Australia and New Zealand from the U.S. and to offer greater protection to the now-vulnerable Pacific Islands, which together formed a key Allied supply chain.

The Battle of the Coral Sea lasted for just four days, and it was the first battle to be fought entirely by fighter planes launched from aircraft carriers, meaning that neither side ever caught sight of the enemy during the whole conflict. After four days of punishing air combat, in which both fleets suffered numerous losses to aircraft and personnel, as well as significant damage to one aircraft carrier on either side, the Allies successfully repelled the Japanese and forced them to abandon their intended advance south.

Midway

After the defeat in the Coral Sea, the Japanese Navy decided to focus its attention on the island of Midway, a small atoll that as the name suggests, is found approximately halfway between the U.S. mainland and Asia. It was considered to be of key strategic importance to both sides, and ever since the losses of Guam and Wake Island, it had become America's most westerly possession left in the Pacific as well as an important submarine refuelling base. From a Japanese point of view, Midway represented a win/win opportunity: they could extend their strategic position even further east by overpowering the small defensive garrison on the island, and also attack the U.S. Navy's Pacific Fleet when it inevitably came to the island's rescue.

U.S. Intelligence managed to foil the element of surprise once again, giving Admiral Chester Nimitz, Commander-in-Chief of the Pacific Fleet, time to manoeuvre all of his available assets as near as possible to Midway. Knowing the exact time at which the attack was planned to start meant that instead of the aircraft at Midway being sitting ducks on the airport tarmac, they were all up in the air when the first Japanese bombers arrived and were able to engage with them from the outset. The Japanese assault began at 4.30am on 4th June 1942, and despite scoring several direct hits on the island's fuel tanks and buildings, crucially the airport runways remained operational. This battle would again be fought mainly from aircraft carriers, and Japan counted on four of their own, in comparison to the U.S. Navy's three, although as long as the Japanese were unable to eliminate Midway Airfield, the island effectively acted as a fourth. The U.S. Navy's torpedo bombers, the Douglas Devastators, had performed admirably at the Battle of the Coral Sea by operating close to the water's surface and had successfully destroyed one of the Japanese aircraft carriers. At Midway they performed noticeably worse - they were slower and less manoeuvrable than their Japanese counterparts and failed to score a single torpedo hit on the enemy.

However, with the Imperial Navy unable to launch their usual number of aeroplanes due to the threat of the torpedo bombers, the U.S. Navy dive bombers were free to achieve direct hits on three Japanese aircraft carriers, each one packed with fully fuelled aircraft. With three of Japan's four carriers now burning wrecks, it was left to the crew of the *Hiryu* to single-handedly lead the attack, which they did by launching two waves of bombers against the U.S. Pacific Fleet, one of which sank the aircraft carrier, USS *Yorktown*. However, revenge was exacted within a few hours when a squadron of American aircraft attacked and badly damaged the *Hiryu*, forcing the Japanese to scuttle her early the next morning.

Several Japanese cruisers and submarines remained in the waters around Midway, but with all four of their aircraft carriers now lying on the sea floor, the U.S. Navy had struck a mortal blow. At 3am on 5th June, the Japanese authorities called off the entire invasion and retreated west; they had lost 2,500 men compared to the Allies' 307, and 322 planes to the Americans' 147. It had been a chastening defeat for the Imperial Navy and marked a decisive shift in the direction of the war, ending the string of Japanese victories that had begun in Pearl Harbour and continued throughout Southeast Asia as far west as Sri Lanka. The importance of the victory was not lost on Admiral Nimitz either, who was positive enough after the victory to give this optimistic assessment: '*Pearl Harbor has now been partially avenged. Vengeance will not be complete until Japanese sea power has been reduced to impotence. We have made substantial progress in that direction. Perhaps we will be forgiven if we claim we are about midway (!) to our objective.*' The American victory at Midway also shifted the balance of naval power in the Pacific, and the Allied forces were finally able to go on the offensive for the first time during the war. It was agreed that they would stage land assaults on Guadalcanal in the Solomon Islands and the Japanese-occupied half of New Guinea, with the aim of penetrating the defensive perimeter that Japan had established in the Southwest Pacific.

Guadalcanal

Allied Intelligence had learned that the Japanese were building an airstrip on Guadalcanal, the main island of the Solomon Islands, and it became of paramount importance to take control of the island before the Japanese could obtain a further foothold in the western Pacific. Allied troops were despatched to Guadalcanal and New Guinea in a two-pronged attack that would support the predominantly Australian soldiers based on both islands, who were valiantly trying to halt the Imperial Army's advance. The Battle of Guadalcanal began two months after the victory at Midway and raged on for six arduous months. It was a brutal conflict in which every branch of the U.S. military participated – the Army, Navy, Coast Guard, and Marines (the U.S. Air Force had not yet been founded as an independent service, and it remained part of the Army until 1947) – and losses on all sides were considerable. The conditions on the ground were also like nothing the Allied forces had ever faced before, with searing heat accompanied by tropical downpours and unbearable humidity. Many of the

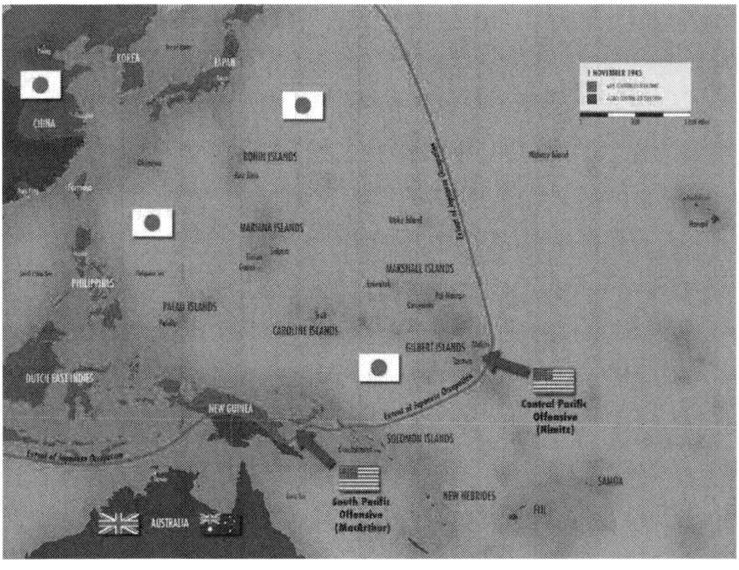

troops had been sent to the Pacific after only a few weeks of basic training, and diseases such as malaria and dengue fever were so prevalent on these islands that they caused as many deaths as the fighting itself. However, despite numerous operational setbacks, Guadalcanal represented the first time during the war that the Allies had mounted an offensive strike against the Japanese, and it was to be an important foreshadowing for the way in which the rest of the war would play out.

Amphibious invasions by the U.S. Marines successfully captured the strategically important airfield on Guadalcanal, and it was renamed Henderson Field after one of their officers who had been killed at Midway. However, it took until early 1943 for the Allies to finally repel the Japanese attacks on Guadalcanal and New Guinea, and both sides paid an extremely high price in human lives. On one night alone, the Japanese surprised ten Allied warships anchored in the passage between Guadalcanal and Savo Island and torpedoed five of them to the bottom of the sea, taking 1,270 men with them. That stretch of water is now known as Iron Bottom Sound due to the 200 ships and almost 700 aircraft belonging to both sides found scattered across the sea floor.

Other islands in the Solomon and New Guinea groups were also recaptured by the Allies, who took advantage of an exhausted Japanese military that had been fighting a campaign lasting almost two years without any respite. The senior officers of the Imperial Army had drawn up an extremely ambitious invasion plan for the Pacific, starting in Hawai'i but covering everywhere from Southeast Asia and Australia to the Aleutian Islands in Alaska. They seemingly never expected the scale of the Allied resistance that they met, and losses to both their personnel and machinery were occurring at much greater rates than they could ever be replaced. Their overextended troops were simply unable to deal with the Allied offensive on so many fronts, and combined with the superior code-breaking skills that American Intelligence enjoyed, this resulted in the highest number of casualties of any WW2 Theatre. In November 1943, U.S. forces retook the Gilbert Islands (modern-day Kiribati), followed soon after by the Marshall Islands, both of which had been important strategic strongholds for the Japanese up until then. By 1944, the momentum of the war in the Pacific had clearly swung towards the Allies, and they were able to gradually advance towards the Asian mainland thanks to a succession of victories in Guam, Saipan, Palau, and the Philippines. However, retaking each of these islands came at an extremely high price, and people have since questioned the rationale behind engaging with every single Japanese garrison, even on minor islands. Battles such as those on Tarawa and later Guam would claim the lives of over 5,000 and 20,000 soldiers respectively, as well as hundreds of innocent civilians.

While the American victory at Midway had ensured the long-term safety of Hawai'i, the same protection was also extended to the rest of Polynesia, which now found itself sufficiently far from the battlegrounds of the Southwest Pacific. Allied garrisons had been established in Tonga, Samoa, and Fiji, and some countries such as the Cook Islands had even set up their own local defence forces, although none of these were ever called into action. The strategic importance of the Pacific Islands at that time was to maintain a continuous supply and communications chain between America and Australasia, and each individual island served as a vital connector in that process. Isolating Australia and New Zealand by themselves would have made it much easier for Japan to capture both, and thus given them greater control over the entire region by leaving the Allies with no friendly bases in the western Pacific.

The U.S. Navy did use one island in French Polynesia for a supply station and built the country's first and only airstrip on the magnificent island of Bora Bora, later to serve as French Polynesia's main international airport until 1960. Almost 7,000 American soldiers were stationed on the island for the duration of the war, with an array of 7-inch guns placed strategically around the coastline in case of a Japanese attack. Eight of those guns are still found in their original positions today and look completely incongruous in an otherwise paradisiacal setting. One of the reasons why people struggle to fully grasp the horrors of the Pacific War while touring the former battlefields today is that they are generally all now pristine islands that are the very embodiments of idyllic tranquillity. This fact contributes greatly to the Pacific Theatre never having earned the same global notoriety as the European battles of WW2, where sites such as Normandy and Dunkirk have been immortalised forever.

The Atomic Finale

While America's participation in the Second World War began with the surprise attack on Pearl Harbour, its final combative act also had its origins in the Pacific, in this case on the tiny island of Tinian in Micronesia. As one of the three Northern Mariana Islands, Tinian was recaptured by the U.S. Marines in July 1944 and was soon converted into the largest air base of the entire war, with six full-size runways constructed especially for the American bomber fleet. Given the island's proximity to the Japanese mainland, Tinian became the ideal home for the hundreds of B-29 bombers stationed in the Western Pacific. The long-range capabilities of the B-29s finally allowed for direct raids on Tokyo, with each mission from Tinian taking approximately 12 hours round trip, and by early 1945 the U.S. Army Air Force was wreaking havoc on the Japanese capital. In February it was decided that Tinian would become the base for a final atomic offensive against Japan, in the belief that it would take 50 atomic bombs to defeat the enemy once and for all. At the time, atomic devices were considered to be little more than large-scale conventional weapons, and with limited understanding about their potency and the long-term effects of radiation, their use was much less questioned than would certainly be the case today.

In July 1945, President Harry Truman issued the Potsdam

Declaration, demanding the unconditional surrender of the Imperial Armed Forces and threatening Japan with 'prompt and utter destruction' in the event of their not doing so. When the Japanese rejected this ultimatum three days later, the components for the first two atomic bombs were dispatched to Tinian, and their assembly began soon after. On 5th August, a B-29 was manoeuvred over a specially constructed loading pit on the island's North Airfield, and the oversized uranium atomic device, known as 'Little Boy', loaded into its weapons bay. The following morning, Little Boy became the first atomic bomb ever to be used in warfare when it was dropped on the city of Hiroshima, causing previously-unimaginable destruction. Three days later, another atomic bomb was released over the city of Nagasaki, this time using a plutonium device nicknamed 'Fat Man'. The target for this second bombing had originally been the city of Kokura, where the Japanese had one of their largest munitions factories, but poor weather over the city on the morning of 9th August meant the crew of the B-29 instead diverted to their back-up site. Both Hiroshima and Nagasaki were flattened to a large degree, and Japanese civilian casualties numbered about 200,000 from both explosions, with many more dying in subsequent years from radiation exposure.

On 10th August 1945, the Japanese sent the Allies the briefest of messages via morse code: 'Japan Accepts Potsdam Proclamation.' The popular narrative today is that the effects of the two atomic bombs, coupled with preparations by the U.S. for further bombings the following week, led to the immediate end of the Pacific War and the final military action of WW2. However, historians now agree that while Hiroshima and Nagasaki were both serious setbacks, the cumulative bombings of Tokyo were in fact much more damaging than either in terms of human casualties and the loss of infrastructure. In truth, it was the entry of the Soviet Union into the war on 9th August that proved to be the knockout blow, since Japan knew that they were unable to fight against two superpowers at the same time. The Soviet Union had previously signed a neutrality pact with Japan in April 1941, but upon learning of the Japanese Emperor's refusal to surrender despite the demise of Hitler and thus prolonging WW2, the Soviet Government was left with no choice but to declare war on their former allies.

The Japanese announced their unconditional surrender on 15th August 1945, and the formal Instrument of Surrender was signed on board the flagship of the Pacific Fleet, USS *Missouri*, on 2nd September in Tokyo Bay. It brought an end to one of the most brutal conflicts in human history, and one which had claimed the lives of approximately 2 million Japanese and 300,000 Allied troops. One of the most enduring images of war was captured during the particularly fierce fighting that took place in early 1945 on the island of Iwo Jima, although on this occasion the American casualties outnumbered those of their enemy. Nevertheless, the exact moment when six U.S. Marines raised the American flag on top of Mount Suribachi was captured by the war photographer Joe Rosenthal, and quickly became one of the most emblematic pictures of WW2 and of Allied resilience anywhere. It was an evocative image of American troops fighting a war thousands of miles from their home, and it was made even more poignant by the fact that only three of the six Marines featured in the photograph ever returned home.

Fortunately, international conflict has not returned to the Pacific Ocean since the end of WW2 and nearly all nations in the region have now signed up to the Rarotonga Treaty (South Pacific Nuclear Free Zone), meaning that it should be impossible for the events described in this chapter ever to be repeated. Instead, the main threat currently facing the Pacific Islands is without doubt an environmental one, and the extent to which climate change and rising sea levels worsen will ultimately dictate the habitability of large parts of the Pacific. The government of Kiribati has already purchased land in Fiji in order to safeguard the future of its food production or repatriate its population, in the event of its own

islands becoming submerged. However, many of the key decisions affecting the future of this region will be taken by countries and organizations located thousands of miles away, and often by people with little understanding of the Pacific and its people. One can only hope that this remote corner of our planet will be preserved in a sustainable and intelligent manner, and that these islands will continue to captivate visitors as they have done ever since the Polynesians first set foot here.

About the Author

James Grant-Peterkin was born in Inverness, Scotland and graduated with a degree in Modern Languages from Cambridge University. His studies in Linguistics led him somewhat fortuitously to the South Pacific, where he was instantly captivated by the rich variety of languages and cultures found in the region. He spent 17 years living and working on Easter Island and was the British Honorary Consul there from 2009 to 2023. He is also the author of the guidebook, 'A Companion to Easter Island', which has so far been translated into six languages.

Primarily a cultural historian, James has been a regular lecturer about Polynesia on cruise ships and at schools and universities, and has also contributed written pieces about the Pacific to Chatham House and the BBC. This collection of stories is the first in the 'Travel Enrichment Series', aimed at helping people to get the very most out of their travels with a unique selection of regional history and insight.

For further information about James and to watch his online lectures, visit www.jamesgrantpeterkin.com

Printed in Great Britain
by Amazon

34235578R00112